# Reach Around the World

*52 Global*
*Awareness*
*Activities for*
*Christian*
*Youth*

## BOB AND SANDY FRIESEN

All Bible quotations, unless otherwise indicated, are from the
Holy Bible, New International Version, © 1973, 1978, 1984,
International Bible Society. Used by permission of Zondervan
Bible Publishers.

Cover design: Scott Rattray

ISBN: 1-56476-280-7

1 2 3 4 5 6 7 8 9 10 Printing/Year 98 97 96 95 94

Produced for Victor Books by The Livingstone Corporation.
David Veerman, Michael Kendrick, and Brenda James Todd, pro-

*To our children, Rhyan, Dustin and Natasha, and to youth around the world.*
*To our parents Stanley and Phillys Burns and John and Lucille Friesen.*

*Special thanks to Elaine Colvin for her encouragement and guidance.*
*Special thanks also to Janet Walker for her invaluable assistance with the manuscript.*
*Thanks to Don and Terri Triplett, Ron and Kathy Iwasko,*
*Cary and Faye Tidwell, Bill Eastlake, the MK (missionary kid) staff*
*who work with us each summer,*
*and to the wonderful people at Christ Memorial Church in Poulsbo, WA.*

# INTRODUCTION

### Making Missions Come Alive

The goal with these activities is to help young people experience missions; to go beyond simply learning about missions, to giving them a "feel for missions" through these missions experiences.

### Involvement Learning

The approach is to involve students in these missions experiences by:

A. Involving all their senses: sight and hearing as well as touch, smell, and taste.

B. Involving them as active participants rather than as passive spectators. We want to help them enjoy the activities by having fun and by getting them totally involved.

C. Giving them opportunity to learn through "discovery." When people discover a truth themselves, they take ownership of what they have learned and, therefore, remember it longer.

D. Presenting mission vision to young people weekly.

The emphasis is on helping the young people learn. A person can lecture; but, there is no guarantee of how much the hearers learn. These activities are geared to help kids learn.

### Making It Part of the Youth Program: When to Use

These activities are designed to plug into any part of a youth meeting or class. They can be used at the opening, during songs and worship, as a special segment, as an illustration, as an introduction to a message or lesson, at the end as a challenge, or during the altar service. They can be used in the youth services, Sunday school classes, Bible studies, discipleship groups, retreats, and prayer meetings. The youth leader becomes a facilitator or guide rather than a lecturer when conducting these experiences.

### Creating a Learning Environment: Making It Work

The key is to create a comfortable learning atmosphere—non-competitive, non-threatening, a place where it is okay to make mistakes and okay to be embarrassed. The students have to be taught how to be tolerant and accepting of other people. The following ground rules help set the stage.

A.  Ground Rules

Create a comfortable atmosphere by laying down some basic ground rules. This gives students direction and shows them your expectations.

1.  *No put-downs:* Put-downs embarrass people, making them feel stupid and inferior. Our youth culture's sense of humor thrives on putting others down. Eliminating put-downs is the first step in creating a comfortable learning environment. So, don't allow put-downs, not even of yourself. Encourage everyone to listen for put-downs. When they hear one, they should draw attention to it in a humorous way by announcing, "Put-down, oooooooh! No put-downs." By doing this, they will create a positive peer pressure to help develop a relaxed learning atmosphere.

2.  *Encourage one another:* Instead of put-downs, encourage one another, especially during difficult times when young people make mistakes. Find the good in each person and give compliments.

3.  *Listen:* One person talks at a time; the rest listen. Give full attention to the person talking.

4.  *Follow the Leader:* When explaining an activity, instruct the students that they should not begin the activity until the leader has said "Go." End the activity by using the word "Stop."

B.  Leader's Attitude

The leader's attitude is a major key in creating a comfortable learning environment. Treat all young people equally—no favorites. Accept everyone's feelings as valid. Exercise patience and tolerance. Never put a student down. Use everything to encourage the students—especially their mistakes and embarrassments. Turn everything into a learning experience. An important question to keep before them is, "What have you learned?"

As a leader, be transparent (to the point that it benefits the students), vulnerable, and willing to share. During these activities be a guide, modeler, and facilitator, rather than a lecturer or preacher.

# TABLE OF CONTENTS

# PART I

## *Warm Up to the World*

These activities are designed to energize the group, build their global awareness and increase their missions participation.

# Do You Know Your World?

"Enlarge the place of your tent, stretch your tent curtains wide, do not hold back; lengthen your cords, strengthen your stakes." (Isaiah 54:2)

In small groups, students list as many countries as possible on a nameless map of the world. This is followed by a discussion on needs and the missions effort in selected countries.

## When to Use

- Use as the missions segment for a youth meeting.
- Use to lead into a missions message.
- Use to lead into a prayer time or altar service.

## Objectives

To teach students the names and locations of countries so they can more easily assimilate information about the missions outreach in each country.

To help young people learn more about the missions effort in selected countries to stimulate their interest in participating in various missions efforts.

## Materials

☐ Map of the world without country names. One for each small group (copy the map provided).

☐ Master map with names of countries (provided).

☐ Pencils for each small group.

## Preparation

Copy the maps for the small groups. Decide which countries you want to highlight and gather information about them such as: missionaries in those countries that your church supports, language spoken, percentage of Christians and non-Christians, population of country in major cities, percentage of population under age 15, average wage per month, and so on.[1]

Have your youth workers and interested students research the information regarding each country.

## Method

Have students form into small groups. Give each group a copy of the nameless map of the world and a pencil. Give them two minutes (or more if needed) to pencil in as many names of the countries as they know. Optional: Provide a prize (such as candy or gum) for those groups that have listed the most.

Follow this by discussion regarding the countries you want to highlight. Have those who have researched the information share their findings. Close by challenging your young people about God's call in missions and participating in missions in some other way such as giving, short-term assignments, and so on.

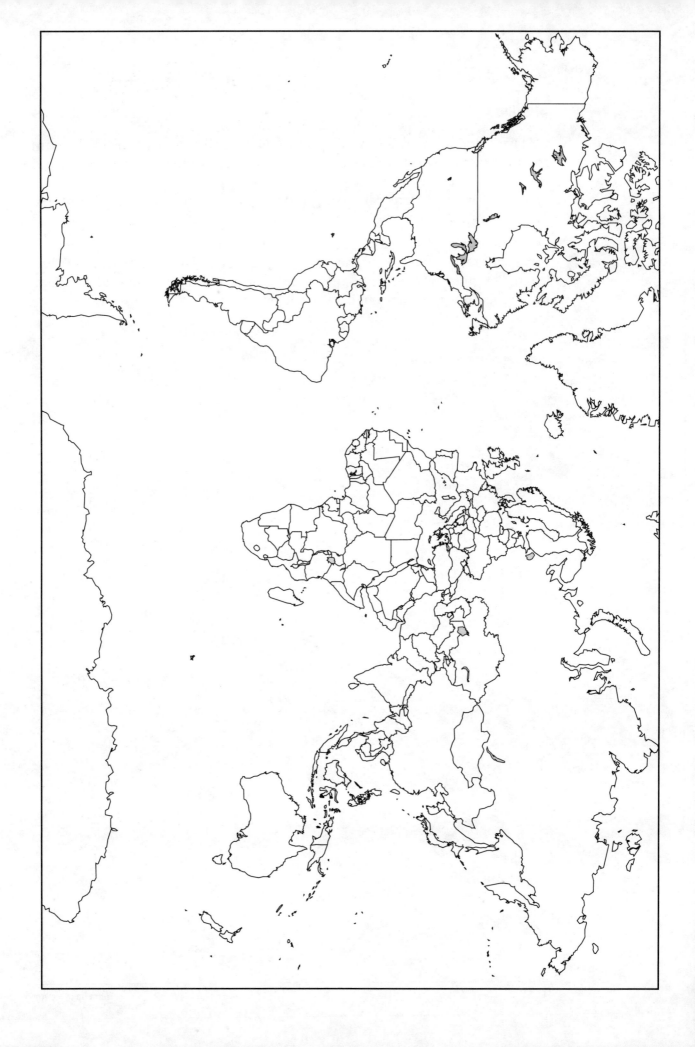

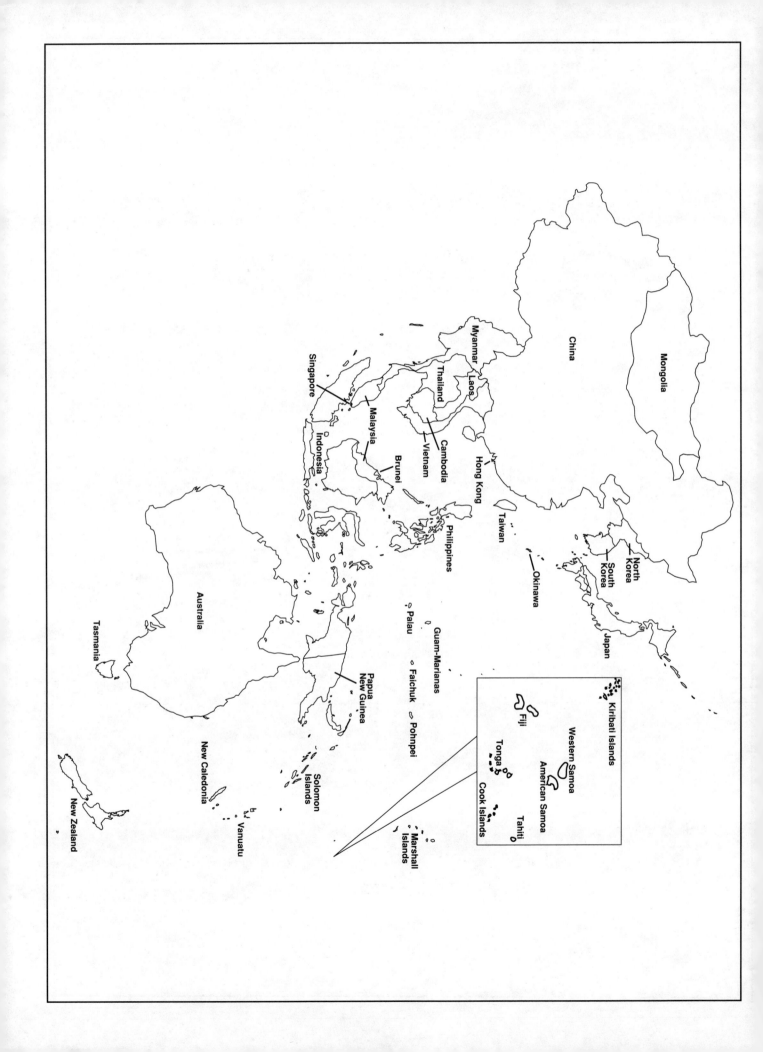

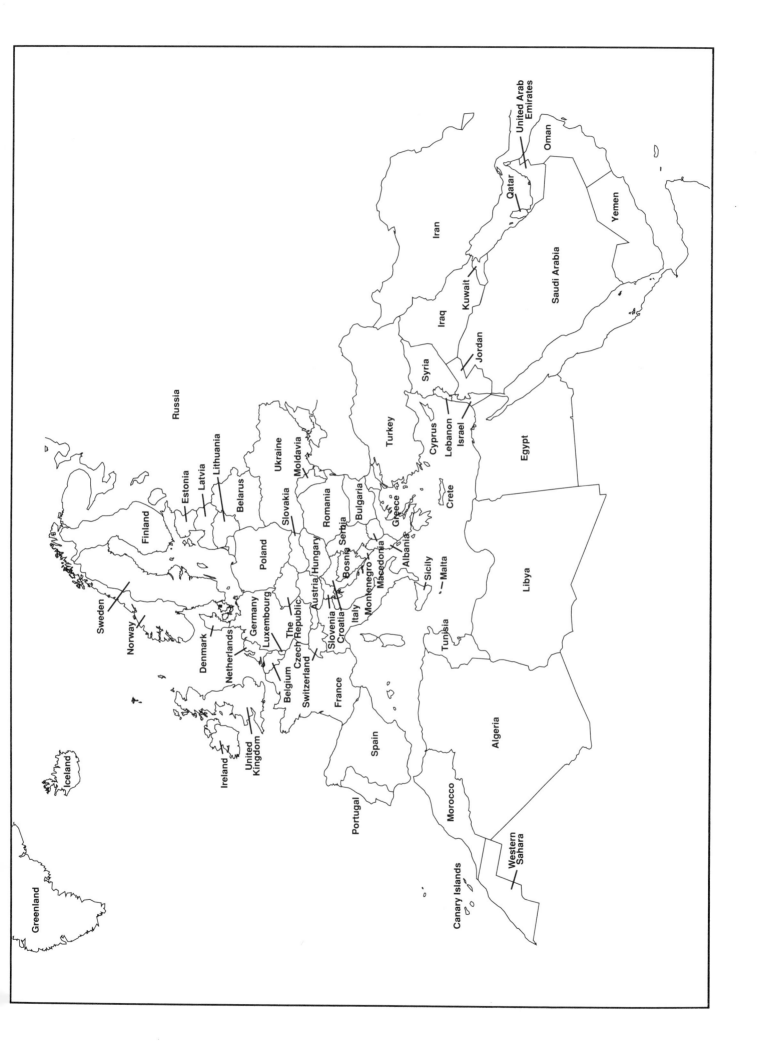

# Introductions

"Go into all the world and preach the good news to all creation." (Mark 16:15)

This activity combines introducing students to each other and introducing unreached people groups to the students.

## When to Use

- Use to begin the meeting.
- Use as an introduction to your message.
- Use as a means to begin a prayer service.
- Use to lead into an altar service or commitment to missions.

## Objective

To help students learn about unreached people groups in order that they may realize the people's need to hear the Word of God.

To challenge young people to become involved in reaching these people with the Word of God through prayer, financial support, or going overseas.

## Materials

☐ 1. List: "Our Globe's 170 Least Evangelized Megapeoples."

☐ 2. 3" x 5" cards—one per student.

## Method

Turn to the list, "Our Globe's 170 Least Evangelized Megapeoples." Transfer the information onto the 3" x 5" cards—one people group per card.

For Example:
1,080,000 Bedouins
living in Egypt

Hand out one card per student as they arrive.

When the group is assembled, have the students introduce themselves and the people group they represent. Each student should stand, give his own name, then the name, number, and country of his people group. Then he introduces the person to the right. For example: "I am George Smith and I represent the 1,080,000 Bedouin people in Egypt. Next to me is Angela Freedman who represents the Afshari people." Then the next person does the same. Give them time before the activity to get acquainted with their neighbors.

As the students give the population figures for each people group, designate one person to total up the figures, so at the end of the activity you can report the total number of countries and total population of least evangelized people groups.

At an appropriate time, gather for prayer focusing on these people groups. Read Romans 10:14-15:

> "How, then, can they call on the one they have not believed in? And how can they believe in the one of whom they have not heard? And how can they hear without someone preaching to them? And how can they preach unless they are sent? As it is written, 'How beautiful are the feet of those who bring good news!'" (NIV)

Challenge the students to aggressively help get the Word to these people. You can emphasize (1) going as a missionary; (2) supporting a missionary; (3) praying; (4) giving to a relief organization; and (5) giving through a missions organization.

Seal their commitment by gathering for prayer. It's important that the students lead in prayer. Gather in small groups according to continents, languages, races, or randomly. Each person can pray for the people group they represent or shuffle the cards, pass them out again, and have each student pray for the people group on his or her new card. Encourage them to take their cards as a prayer reminder during the week. Some may want to research information about their people group and report to the group the following week.

Modify by simply passing out the people group cards instead of doing the introduction activity.

## Our Globe's 170 Least Evangelized Megapeoples

Peoples over 1 million in population in the year 2000, and 50% or less evangelized.

### Meaning of columns

1. Name of people, anglicized, with any additional or alternate names; together with (in bold italic capitals) name of country in which they reside. Identical people names refer to peoples speaking different mother tongues (see column 2).

2. Autoglossonym: this people's own name, in their own language, for their mother tongue—how the people term their own language. Note that virtually all people spell their language names with a lower-case first letter. English is the only language in the world which capitalizes its autoglossonym (and, in fact, all language names). Names in parentheses are alternates. These are only capitalized if they are anglicized names.

3. Population of this people in mid-1990 (based on World Population Pros-

pects 1988, U.N. 1989).

4. Estimated population of this people in middle of the next decade (based on same U.N. estimates).

### COUNTRY

| People name | Autoglossonym | Pop. 1990 | Pop. 2000 |
|---|---|---|---|
| **AFGHANISTAN** | | | |
| Hazara (Berberi) | hzaragi (Afghan Persian) | 1,060,000 | 1,700,000 |
| Pathan (Pushtun, Afghani) | pashto (pushtu, pakhtu) | 8,620,000 | 13,850,000 |
| Tadzhik | tadzhik (galcha, dari) | 3,920,000 | 6,310,000 |
| Uzbek | uzbek (kypchak) | 880,000 | 1,410,000 |
| **ALGERIA** | | | |
| Algerian Arab | jazairi (maghribi) | 17,700,000 | 23,200,000 |
| Greater Kabyle (Western) | qabayil (senhaja, zwawa) | 1,870,000 | 2,450,000 |
| Hamyan Bedouin | badawi (Bedouin Arabic) | 1,770,000 | 2,320,000 |
| **CAMBODIA** | | | |
| Khmer (Cambodian) | khmer (Cambodian) | 6,680,000 | 8,130,000 |
| **CAMEROON** | | | |
| Fula (Adamawa Fulani) | fulfulde (peul) | 970,000 | 1,270,000 |
| **CHAD** | | | |
| Chad Arab | arabiya (Chad Arabic) | 1,460,000 | 1,880,000 |
| **CHINA** | | | |
| Bai (Pai, Minchia) | pai (minchia, minkia) | 1,270,000 | 1,440,000 |
| Central Tibetan (Hsifan) | zang wen (Central Tibetan) | 4,360,000 | 4,940,000 |
| Chinese Tai | Chinese Tai | 1,000,000 | 1,130,000 |
| Eatern Meo (Black, Heh) | ch'ientung miao | 2,050,000 | 2,320,000 |
| Han Chinese (Hainanese) | wanning (Wenchang) | 5,110,000 | 5,790,000 |
| Han Chinese (Hakka) | wukinfu (hakka colloquial) | 14,760,000 | 16,720,000 |
| Han Chinese (Hakka) | sankian (sam kiong) | 4,540,000 | 5,140,000 |
| Han Chinese (Hakka) | kejia (hakka colloquial) | 24,980,000 | 28,290,000 |
| Han Chinese (Hakka) | tingchow | 1,140,000 | 1,290,000 |
| Hani | hani (woni, ho, haw) | 1,190,000 | 1,350,000 |
| Hui (Dungan, Tunya) | kuoyu (Mandarin) | 8,130,000 | 9,210,000 |
| I (Yi, Lolo) | nesu (lolo, i, yi) | 6,140,000 | 6,960,000 |
| Kazakh | hasaka (kazakh) | 930,000 | 1,050,000 |
| Khalka Mongol | khalka (dariganga, urat) | 3,840,000 | 4,350,000 |
| Manchu | sibo (manchu, juchen) | 4,840,000 | 5,480,000 |
| Northern Meo (Huayuan) | hsianghsi meo (chiwei) | 1,000,000 | 1,130,000 |
| Nosu | nosu | 1,140,000 | 1,290,000 |
| Puyi (Bouyei, Pu-I) | chungchia (dioijui,igen) | 2,390,000 | 2,700,000 |
| Tujia (Tuchia) | tuchia | 3,190,000 | 3,610,000 |
| Tung (Dong, Kam) | kam (tung-chia, tong) | 1,610,000 | 1,820,000 |
| Uighur (Kashgar) | wei wuer (i-kha, lop) | 6,710,000 | 7,600,000 |
| Western Meo (Peh, Hwa) | ch'uanch'ientien miao | 2,620,000 | 2,960,000 |
| Yaoyao (mien, man, taipan) | | 1,580,000 | 1,790,000 |
| Zhuang (Chuang, Chwang) | chwang (chuang, yungpei) | 15,070,000 | 17,060,000 |

| COUNTRY | | | |
|---|---|---|---|
| People name | Autoglossonym | Pop. 1990 | Pop. 2000 |

**EGYPT**

| People name | Autoglossonym | Pop. 1990 | Pop. 2000 |
|---|---|---|---|
| Arabized Berber | masri (mashriqi) | 1,070,000 | 1,300,000 |
| Bedouin | badawi (Bedouin Arabic) | 1,080,000 | 1,330,000 |
| Halebi Gypsy | masri (mashriqi) | 860,000 | 1,070,000 |

**ETHIOPIA**

| People name | Autoglossonym | Pop. 1990 | Pop. 2000 |
|---|---|---|---|
| Somali | somali (soomaali) | 2,450,000 | 3,210,000 |

**GUINEA**

| People name | Autoglossonym | Pop. 1990 | Pop. 2000 |
|---|---|---|---|
| Fula Jalon (Futa Dyalon) | futa jalo (pulaar) | 1,920,000 | 2,480,000 |
| Maninka (South Malinke) | maninka (manding, malinke) | 1,740,000 | 2,240,000 |
| Susa (Soso) | soso (susu) | 790,000 | 1,030,000 |

**INDIA**

| People name | Autoglossonym | Pop. 1990 | Pop. 2000 |
|---|---|---|---|
| Bagri (Bahgri) | bagri (baorias) | 1,640,000 | 2,010,000 |
| Central Bhil | bhili (Bhilori) | 3,940,000 | 4,820,000 |
| Central Gond (Ghond) | mandla gondi | 850,000 | 1,040,000 |
| Deccani (Dakhini Hindi) | dakhini (deccan, dakni) | 11,790,000 | 14,400,000 |
| Dogri (Hindi Dogri) | dogri (dhogaryali, bhatholi) | 1,850,000 | 2,260,000 |
| Eatern Bhil (Vil) | dehwali bhili (bhilbari) | 2,370,000 | 2,900,000 |
| Garhwali (Central Pahari) | tehri | 860,000 | 1,060,000 |
| Garhwali (Pahari Gashwali) | srinagaria (gadwahi) | 1,140,000 | 1,390,000 |
| Hindustani | hindustani | 870,000 | 1,070,000 |
| Ho | ho (lanka kol, lohara) | 1,170,000 | 1,430,000 |
| Kashmiri (Keshur) | kashmiri (poguli, rambani) | 3,770,000 | 4,610,000 |
| Kortha Bihari | kortha magahi | 1,710,000 | 2,090,000 |
| Kui (Khondi, Kond) | kui (khand, kodu, kodulu) | 2,560,000 | 3,130,000 |
| Kumaoni (Central Pahari) | kumauni (kumgoni) | 1,920,000 | 2,350,000 |
| Lamani (Banjara, Labhani) | lamani (lambadi, kora) | 1,870,000 | 2,290,000 |
| Malvi (Uijaini, Malavi) | malavi (bachadi, patvi) | 1,000,000 | 1,230,000 |
| Manipuri (Meithei, Kathe) | manipuri (ponna) | 1,220,000 | 1,490,000 |
| Mina | mina | 2,240,000 | 2,740,000 |
| Nagpuri Bihari (Sadri) | sadan (nagpuri, dikkukaji) | 1,900,000 | 2,320,000 |
| Nepalese (Gurkhali) | khas kura (nepali, palpa) | 2,000,000 | 2,450,000 |
| Nimadi (Nimari) | nimadi (nemadi, bhuani) | 1,240,000 | 1,510,000 |
| North Central Gond | chhindwara gondi | 880,000 | 1,090,000 |
| Northern Gond (Betul) | betul gondu (koitor, gandi) | 850,000 | 1,040,000 |
| Rajasthani (Bikaneri) | bikaneri | 860,000 | 1,070,000 |
| Rajasthani (Mewari) | mewari | 840,000 | 1,030,000 |
| Sindhi (Kachchi,, Bhatia) | sindhi (lari, thareli) | 1,880,000 | 2,290,000 |
| Southern Bhil | valvi bhili | 1,120,000 | 1,360,000 |
| Tulu (Tullu, Thulu, Tal) | tulu (tilu, tuluva bhasa) | 1,800,000 | 2,200,000 |
| Wagdi (Wagheri, Vagdi) | wagdi (vagi, wagholi) | 1,470,000 | 1,800,000 |

**INDONESIA**

| People name | Autoglossonym | Pop. 1990 | Pop. 2000 |
|---|---|---|---|
| Achehnese (Aceh, Atjeh) | aceh (banda, daja, pase) | 3,020,000 | 3,490,000 |
| Banjarese | banjar | 1,440,000 | 1,660,000 |
| Bazaar Low Malay Creole | pasar melayu (Bazaar, Low) | 1,260,000 | 1,460,000 |
| Buginese (Bugis) | bugis | 4,830,000 | 5,580,000 |
| Jambinese Malay (Batin) | jambina (Jambinese) | 1,280,000 | 1,480,000 |
| Komering (Ogan) | komering (ogan) | 1,080,000 | 1,250,000 |
| Lamponger (Lampungese) | lampung (Lampungese) | 1,170,000 | 1,350,000 |
| Madurese | bankalan (Madurese) | 11,330,000 | 13,080,000 |
| Makassarese (Macassar) | macassar (mengkasara) | 3,070,000 | 3,540,000 |

| COUNTRY<br>People name | Autoglossonym | Pop. 1990 | Pop. 2000 |
|---|---|---|---|
| **INDONESIA (cont.)** | | | |
| Malay (Coast Malay) | malay (bahasa malaysia) | 1,810,000 | 2,080,000 |
| Minangkabau | minangkabau | 6,680,000 | 7,710,000 |
| Sasak | sasak | 2,070,000 | 2,390,000 |
| Sundanese | sundanese | 24,550,000 | 28,330,000 |
| **IRAN** | | | |
| Afghan Persian (Kaboli) | dari (kaboli, khorasani) | 1,580,000 | 2,080,000 |
| Afshari (Afsar) | azeri (azerbaijani) | 850,000 | 1,120,000 |
| Azerbaijani (Turk) | azeri (tabris, moqaddan) | 7,160,000 | 9,420,000 |
| Bakhtiari | bakhtiari (luri) | 1,080,000 | 1,410,000 |
| Baluchi | baluchi | 1,240,000 | 1,640,000 |
| Central Kurd | mukri (Eastern Kermanji) | 1,130,000 | 1,490,000 |
| Gilaki | gilaki (gelaki, gilani) | 3,280,000 | 4,320,000 |
| Iranian Arab | arabiya (Iranian Arabic) | 1,190,000 | 1,560,000 |
| Iranian Kurd | farsi (Persian) | 3,400,000 | 4,470,000 |
| Luri (Lori) | luri (feyli, alaki, kelhuri) | 3,230,000 | 4,240,000 |
| Mazanderani | mazanderani (tabri, palari) | 2,600,000 | 3,430,000 |
| Persian (Irani) | farsi (Persian, dari) | 18,900,000 | 24,870,000 |
| Qashqai | qashqai | 860,000 | 1,130,000 |
| Southern Kurd (Carduchi) | kermanshahi (kurdi) | 2,830,000 | 3,720,000 |
| Turkmen (Turkomani) | turkmen (anauli, esari, teke) | 910,000 | 1,190,000 |
| Zott Gypsy (Nawar) | arabiya (Arabic) | 1,080,000 | 1,410,000 |
| **IRAQ** | | | |
| Iraqi Arab | arabiya (Iraqi Arabic) | 12,940,000 | 18,020,000 |
| Iraqi Kurd | arabiya (Iraqi Arabic) | 1,140,000 | 1,580,000 |
| Northern Kurd | kermanji (hakari, jezire) | 2,820,000 | 3,920,000 |
| **IVORY COAST** | | | |
| Malinke (Ivorian) | maninka (south malinke) | 1,390,000 | 2,040,000 |
| Senufo (Minianka) | senari (senadi, tyebara) | 1,140,000 | 1,670,000 |
| **LIBYA** | | | |
| Cyrenaican Arab | barqi (mashriqi) | 1,180,000 | 1,690,000 |
| Tripolitanian Arab | tarabulusi (maghribi) | 1,360,000 | 1,950,000 |
| **MALI** | | | |
| Fula (Peuhala) | massina (fula peuhala) | 830,000 | 1,130,000 |
| **MALAYSIA** | | | |
| Malay (Melaju, Melayu) | malay (bahasa malaysia) | 5,600,000 | 6,740,000 |
| **MAURITANIA** | | | |
| Bidan (White Moor) | hassani (badawi) | 1,040,000 | 1,390,000 |
| **MONGOLIA** | | | |
| Khalka Mongol | khalka (Mongolian) | 1,480,000 | 2,000,000 |
| **MOROCCO** | | | |
| Arabized Berber | maghribi (mogrebi) | 2,140,000 | 2,670,000 |
| Beraber | tamazight (beraber, ksurs) | 2,590,000 | 3,230,000 |

| COUNTRY People name | Autoglossonym | Pop. 1990 | Pop. 2000 |
|---|---|---|---|
| **MOROCCO** *(cont.)* | | | |
| Jebala | maghribi (mogrebi) | 1,080,000 | 1,350,000 |
| Moroccan Arab | maghribi (mogrebi) | 12,600,000 | 15,710,000 |
| Riffian (Northern Shilha) | riff (senhaja, iznacen) | 1,480,000 | 1,850,000 |
| Shleuh | tachelhait (masmudah) | 1,780,000 | 2,230,000 |
| Susiua (Southern Shilha) | susuia (susi, susina) | 1,010,000 | 1,250,000 |
| | | | |
| **MYANMAR** | | | |
| Burmese (Myen) | bama (Burmese) | 26,290,000 | 32,260,000 |
| Burmese Shan (Thai Yai) | shan (ngio, sha) | 2,920,000 | 3,580,000 |
| | | | |
| **NEPAL** | | | |
| Bhojpuri Bihari | bhojpuri | 1,370,000 | 1,730,000 |
| Maitili (tirahutia) | matili | 2,260,000 | 2,850,000 |
| Nepalese (Eastern Pahari) | khas kura (parbatiya) | 9,910,000 | 12,460,000 |
| Tamang (Tamar, Sain) | tamang | 950,000 | 1,190,000 |
| | | | |
| **NIGER** | | | |
| Hausa (Tazarawa) | hausa | 1,490,000 | 2,040,000 |
| Sokoto Fulani | fulfulde niger (sokoto) | 780,000 | 1,070,000 |
| Zerma (dyerma) | zama (dyerma, adzerma) | 1,190,000 | 1,630,000 |
| | | | |
| **NIGERIA** | | | |
| Bororo (Western Fulani) | fulfulde | 1,700,000 | 2,390,000 |
| Fulani (Haabe) | fulfulde (kano-katsina) | 1,920,000 | 2,710,000 |
| Fulani (Toroobe) | hausa (Eastern Hausa) | 5,540,000 | 7,800,000 |
| Hausa | hausa | 18,990,000 | 26,740,000 |
| Kanuri | kanuri | 4,450,000 | 6,270,000 |
| Sokoto Fulani | fulfulde (sokoto) | 1,930,000 | 2,720,000 |
| | | | |
| **NORTH KOREA** | | | |
| Korean | chosenmal (Korean) | 22,720,000 | 27,900,000 |
| | | | |
| **OMAN** | | | |
| Omani Arab | arabiya (Omani Arabic) | 1,060,000 | 1,480,000 |
| | | | |
| **PAKISTAN** | | | |
| Baluchi | baluchi | 3,670,000 | 4,860,000 |
| Brahui | brahui | 910,000 | 1,200,000 |
| Pathan (Afghani, Waziri) | pashto (pushtu, paktu) | 12,480,000 | 16,530,000 |
| Sindhi | sindhi (lari, lasi) | 17,810,000 | 23,590,000 |
| Urdu | urdu | 11,160,000 | 14,780,000 |
| | | | |
| **SAUDI ARABIA** | | | |
| Saudi Arab | arabiya (Saudi Arabic) | 9,290,000 | 13,600,000 |
| Yemeni Arab | arabiya (Yemeni Arabic) | 2,970,000 | 4,340,000 |
| | | | |
| **SENEGAL** | | | |
| Fulakunda (fula Cunda) | fulakunda (pulaar) | 910,000 | 1,200,000 |

| COUNTRY<br>People name | Autoglossonym | Pop. 1990 | Pop. 2000 |
|---|---|---|---|
| **SOMALIA** | | | |
| Sab | somali (sab) | 820,000 | 1,060,000 |
| Somali | somali (somalinya) | 5,940,000 | 7,710,000 |
| | | | |
| **SOUTH YEMEN** | | | |
| Yemeni Arab | arabiya (Yemeni Arabic) | 2,060,000 | 2,830,000 |
| | | | |
| **SOVIET UNION, FORMER REPUBLICS OF** | | | |
| Azerbaijani (Azurbijan) | azeri (azerbaijani) | 6,846,000 | 7,315,000 |
| Bashkir | bashkir (bashkirian) | 1,510,000 | 1,610,000 |
| Kazakh | kazakh (Western Kirghiz) | 8,200,000 | 8,770,000 |
| Kirghiz | kirghiz (kara, Black) | 2,550,000 | 2,730,000 |
| Tadzhik | tadzhik | 4,250,000 | 4,540,000 |
| Tatar (Kazan Tatar) | kazan tatar | 6,700,000 | 7,160,000 |
| Turkmen | turkmen (jagarta) | 2,740,000 | 2,930,000 |
| Uzbek | uzbek | 16,820,000 | 17,970,000 |
| | | | |
| **SRI LANKA** | | | |
| Ceylon Moor | tamil | 1,120,000 | 1,260,000 |
| | | | |
| **SUDAN** | | | |
| Beja (Beni-Amer, Ababda) | bedawye (beja, bedawiya) | 1,160,000 | 1,550,000 |
| Eastern Nuer (Jikany Door) | naath (jikany door) | 820,000 | 1,090,000 |
| Gaaliin | ja'ali (mashriqi-badawi) | 1,690,000 | 2,250,000 |
| Guhayna | kababish (mashriqi-badawi) | 780,000 | 1,040,000 |
| | | | |
| **SYRIA** | | | |
| Bedouin Arab | badawi (Bedouin Arabic) | 930,000 | 1,300,000 |
| Western Kurd (Kermanji) | kermanji (kurdi) | 690,000 | 1,350,000 |
| | | | |
| **THAILAND** | | | |
| Northern Tai (Yuan, Phyap) | tai (kammyang, myang) | 5,300,000 | 6,060,000 |
| Pattani Malay | malay pattani | 930,000 | 1,070,000 |
| Southern Tai (Pak Thai) | tai orkhon (Southern) | 3,120,000 | 3,560,000 |
| | | | |
| **TUNISIA** | | | |
| Sahel Bedouin | badawi (Bedouin Arabic) | 1,750,000 | 2,100,000 |
| Tunisian Arab | ifriqi (maghribi) | 5,460,000 | 6,570,000 |
| | | | |
| **TURKEY** | | | |
| Crimean Tatar | turkce (Turkish) | 3,890,000 | 4,660,000 |
| Northern Kurd (Kermanji) | zaza (dimli, gurmanji) | 5,010,000 | 6,000,000 |
| Turk | turkce (Turkish) | 38,670,000 | 46,320,000 |
| Turkish Kurd | turkce (Turkish) | 4,450,000 | 5,330,000 |
| | | | |
| **VIET NAM** | | | |
| Khmer (Cambodian) | khmer (Cambodian) | 1,030,000 | 1,270,000 |

Source: P. J. Johnstone, D. B. Barnett, and T. M. Johnson, International Journal of Frontier Missions. Vol. 7:4 Oct. 1990, p133-134. Used with permission.

# Heart for Missions

"The Spirit of the Lord is on me, because he has anointed me to preach good news." (Luke 4:18)

This activity provides a way for young people to share their experiences, knowledge, and desires about missions. It creates a setting for them to be open and honest.

## When To Use

- Use this activity as an introduction to a message.
- Use it to promote missions awareness as a complete missions segment within a youth meeting.
- Use it to challenge young people for a deeper commitment or to be open to missions as a follow-up to a message.
- Use the idea to promote a particular missions event or program such as a local home missions trip. Create your own "Heart for Missions" statements to fit the program you are promoting.

## Objectives

To create a pleasant atmosphere for students to mingle and get acquainted so they will feel comfortable in sharing their interests, experiences, and knowledge about missions.

To help students discover commonality with others regarding missions desires and experience that will encourage them to be more open and honest in sharing.

To challenge students to be open to what God is doing in their lives regarding missions so that they may develop a stronger commitment.

## Materials

☐ Copies of the "Heart for Missions" form (at end of lesson). Make one copy per person.

☐ Pencils—one per person.

## Preparation

Read through the "Heart for Missions" form to familiarize yourself with the statements and terms such as "people group," "mission field," etc. Make copies of the "Heart for Missions" sheet and provide enough pencils for everyone.

## Method

At the designated time during the meeting, hand out the "Heart for Missions" forms and pencils. Tell the students to keep the forms upside down and not to begin until you say "Go."

Before beginning, explain that at some time or another everyone in the room has probably wanted to travel the world. Some have even wanted to live in a foreign country, while others have wanted to be missionaries, or some even may have wanted to help people in foreign countries in other areas like medicine, education, agriculture, or construction. Some students may want to seek a career in foreign countries or just do a short-term assignment. Some students may not be interested in going outside the United States at all. In this activity, young people will discover some of the missions experience, desire, and knowledge of others in the group. (You may need to modify these instructions to fit your students.)

Explain that the students should obtain as many signatures as possible within a time frame. They do this by walking around the room finding other students to sign their "Heart for Missions" forms. At the same time, they will be signing forms for other students. The young people are to put their signature next to statements that apply to them. Each person may sign twice. However, you may want to change the number of signatures a person can sign depending on your group. For a large group, one signature per person may be sufficient. For a smaller group, two or three signatures per person may be needed.

Allow two to four minutes, depending on your group. If they are interacting beyond just exchanging signatures and are exchanging information about themselves, you may want to lengthen the time a bit.

Answer any questions students may have before the activity begins. Start with the word "Go." During that activity, you and other youth sponsors may have to help those who are shy or are having problems getting signatures. At the appropriate time, end the activity and have everyone take their seats.

At this point, find out how many signatures the students got by asking, "How many got signatures for every statement?" Or, "How many of you have signatures for every statement except one . . . two . . . three?" and so forth. When you get down to 10 to 15 unsigned statements, ask "How many still needed 10 or more signatures?" This will minimize embarrassing anyone and give recognition to those who collected the most signatures. Next, begin asking some specifics about the statements which the students signed. This will give you insights into their desires and vision about missions. "How many signed the statement, 'Someone who would like to begin a new work among an unreached people group?'" Then ask those who raised their hands, "Tell us about what you'd like to do . . . Which group? . . . Do you feel called? . . . How did this desire start? . . . etc." If no one answers, move on to another statement.

This process will help you identify those interested in missions and will help young people see each other's vision for missions. Use this time to cultivate new ground for missions outreach among your students. You may want to focus especially on young people who do not participate in missions in any way.

# HEART FOR MISSIONS

This is a person-to-person heart search. Walk around the room collecting signatures from those who match the statements below. Have them sign their name on the line next to the statement that applies to them. This is your chance to get to know everyone here. At the same time, you will be asked to sign statements, too. Each person may sign twice. By the end of this activity, you will discover those who have a heart for missions and you may discover your own heart for missions.

1.  Someone who wants to visit a foreign country. _____
2.  Someone who wants to go on a short-term missions trip overseas. _____
3.  Someone who has participated in a short-term missions trip overseas. _____
4.  Someone who has traveled overseas. _____
5.  Someone who knows the name of the country without a missionary from your denomination. _____
6.  Someone who likes to try exotic foods. _____
7.  Someone who participates in a missions organization. _____
8.  Someone who is called to be a missionary. _____
    What country? _____
9.  Someone who prays for missionaries consistently. _____
10. Someone who supports a missionary. _____ Who? _____
11. Someone who knows a missionary. _____ Who? _____
12. Someone who is interested in learning a foreign language. _____
    Language? _____
13. Someone who loves traveling. _____
14. Someone who likes adventure. _____
15. Someone who wants to preach in a foreign country. _____
16. Someone who wants to preach in a foreign language. _____
17. Someone who wants to be an evangelist on the mission field. _____
18. Someone who wants to begin a new work among an unreached people group. _____
19. Someone who wants to go on a short-term missions assignment after high school. _____
20. Someone who wants to work in a foreign country as a nurse, doctor, teacher, builder, agricultural assistant, etc. _____
21. Someone who wants to help an underprivileged child in another country. _____
22. Someone who would like to build churches overseas. _____
23. Someone who has been in a foreign country. _____
    Where? _____
24. Someone who likes to read about foreign cultures and foreign places. _____ What is your favorite? _____

# Name Tag Creations

"You are the light of the world. . . ." (Matthew 5:14)

Students are provided with blank name tags. They are to write their names on the tag and then draw a sketch of something foreign. After their sketches are completed, they share its meaning with other students. This builds students' world awareness and gives them an opportunity to express themselves.

## When to Use

- Use this activity to help students focus on the message for the meeting.
- Use this at a retreat or special service.
- Use this as a springboard to launch a new project or outreach trip.

## Objective

To provide a creative atmosphere where students are encouraged to think and share about the world. Their interaction will help build their world awareness.

## Materials

- ☐ Adhesive name tags—one per person.
- ☐ Fine-point color markers (preferably water washable) in a variety of colors.

## Preparation

Set up a "name tag" table with the name tags and markers laid out on it.

Arrange chairs in circles of four to eight depending on the overall size of the youth group. Choose a theme for the students to use for the drawings they will put on their name tags. You and your sponsors should create your own name tags before the meeting, so that you will be free to help the students during the activity.

## Method

Distribute the name tags and markers after all have gathered and taken their seats. Hand out one set of markers to each group (be sure there is at least one marker per person). Tell students not to put their names on the tags yet. Explain that they will be creating their own name tags, but these will be more than just name tags. Every person is to have two things on his or her tag.

    1. First and last name.

    2. A sketch of the theme for the evening.

Here are some ideas of what they could draw:

Foreign place they would like to visit.

People praying for a specific need.

A missionary family.

A national family.

A symbol of missions.

What missionaries do overseas. (For example, preaching, building churches, etc.)

A scene from a foreign country.

An object from a foreign country.

An outline of a country or continent.

Future dreams, desires, or goals as they relate to missions.

As students work on their name tags, you and your youth sponsors will need to mill around helping some students with ideas for sketches. Some will be embarrassed to draw and will need encouragement. Allow five minutes, then have everyone share about their name tag creations with the small group. Allow one minute per person. When the groups have finished sharing, ask if anyone would like to share with the entire group. If not, encourage them to share by explaining your own name tag creation.

# People Groups

"But when he saw the multitudes, he was moved with compassion on them. . . ." (Matthew 9:36)

This activity simulates how cultures tend to group together, and it will heighten students' awareness of people groups.

## When to Use

- Use to create an interest for the meeting.
- Use as an icebreaker to help young people get acquainted with each other.
- Use as part of an orientation for a missions trip, short-term missions trip, work day in an ethnic part of the city, etc.

- Use the activity to introduce your message and the statistical information at the end of your message to challenge students for financial support or other means of reaching these people groups.

## Objectives

To provide an opportunity for students to feel what it is like to enter another culture so they can recognize the differences in people groups.

To educate students about the vast number of unreached people groups. As a result they will be challenged to become involved in helping to reach these people groups with the gospel.

## Materials

☐ None.

## Preparation

Clear an area large enough for the entire group to be able to mill around comfortably.

## Method

Have each participant choose an animal that lives on a farm, like a pig, cow, horse, duck, cat, chicken, etc. They must not tell anyone what animal they have chosen.

When you say the word "Go," instruct the students to close their eyes (no peeking), make the sound of the animal they have chosen, and move around the room finding others of the same "species."

As a leader, watch what happens as the students gather together with those of the same sound. Some will be embarrassed, others shy, outgoing, loud, quiet, enthusiastic, etc. You may notice some peeking. When everyone is clustered together in their animal groups, call out, "Stop." There may be one or two loners that never make contact, or there may be two groups of the same animal. Have them open their eyes and stand still.

Ask:

1. How did it feel to be blindly searching for someone making the same sound?

2. How did it feel when you found another person of the same species?

3. How did it feel being alone?

4. How many peeked? Why?

5. What other things did you feel?

Comment on how this is similar to the way people feel when they enter another culture for the first time. Some are shy, while others are outgoing.

At this point you may want them to be seated. Explain how this activity is representative of cultural groups. People naturally gather with others who have many things in common. The term "people groups" is used to designate different cultural groups. For example, in the United States, some of the people groups are Hispanics, African Americans, Muslims, etc.

Below is a statistical listing of the unreached, unevangelized, and languages without the Bible.

**Definitions:**

Unreached—Never heard the gospel or never had the opportunity to contact an indigenous church or fellowship in one's own culture.

Unevangelized—Not had an adequate opportunity to hear the gospel or respond to it; persons who are unaware of Christianity, Christ, and the gospel; those who have never heard the name of Jesus.

Unreached Megapeoples  150
*(Megapeoples–An ethnic group speaking the same mother tongue whose population is over one million.)*

Unreached Micropeoples  50,000
*(Micropeople–A small, close-knit, homogenous population segment.)*

Unreached people groups  12,000
*(People group–significantly large grouping of people who perceive themselves to have common affinity through shared language, religion, ethnicity, residence, occupation, class, caste, situation, etc., or a combination of these.)*

|  | **1990** | **2000** |
| --- | --- | --- |
| Unevangelized population | 1.25 billion | 1.03 billion |
| Unreached peoples with no churches | 450 | 200 |
| Unevangelized percentage of world population | 23.6% | 16.6% |

| | |
| --- | --- |
| Languages | 15,000 |
| Languages without Scripture | 9,100 |
| Languages with only a portion of Scripture | 5,582 |
| Languages with complete Bible | 318 |

Use these statistics along with appropriate Scripture verses to challenge the students to help reach these unreached and unevangelized people groups.

Source: David B. Barrett and Todd M. Johnson, *Our Globe and How to Reach It: Seeing the World Evangelized by A.D. 2000 and Beyond* (Birmingham, Ala.: New Hope,1990).

See also: "Our Globe's 170 Least Evangelized Megapeoples" pages 13-18.

# Plunge Into Missions

"Trust in the Lord with all thine heart; and lean not unto thine own understanding." (Proverbs 3:5)

This activity helps students understand the partnership between supporters and missionaries. One person does the "Nestea plunge" into the arms of eight other students. This involves teamwork and trust.

### When to Use

- Use this activity to challenge young people to be faithful in giving their faith promise general pledges to missionaries, and/or specific mission programs such as child care, relief, etc.

- Use to help young people who are involved with an upcoming missions trip to build trust in their supporters and God.

- Use to begin a meeting.

- Use to introduce a message.

- Use to illustrate a point in a message.

- Use with small groups at a special meeting such as a retreat or discipleship class. Have everyone in each group take the plunge. It is important to have an experienced adult supervise each group.

### Objectives

To teach students the essential relationship between trust and faithfulness and help them apply it to the relationship between supporters and missionaries.

To inform students of the support system the denomination uses in its missions effort so that they will understand the importance of their role in sending missionaries.

### Materials

- ☐ Nine responsible young people.
- ☐ One chair.

### Preparation

If you have never done this activity before, it may be good to practice before the service with some young people. Make sure you know the instructions. It is crucial that the young people follow your every word. The

---

instructions can be given to the young people in front of the large group. It works quite well to ask for volunteers, give them the instructions, and do the activity.

## Method

Ask for volunteers. Pick nine responsible young people, both guys and girls. Gather them around you and explain to them that they are going to perform the "Nestea Plunge." One person is going to stand on a chair with their back to the others. (Choose one of the more adventuresome young people to do the "plunge.") The other eight students will be arranged in such a way as to catch the person taking the plunge.

Stress to your volunteers the importance of following your instructions exactly. Instruct the "catchers" to face each other in two lines of four. They should be directly across from their counterpart with hands stretched out and palms up. Their hands should be able to touch the elbows of the person across from them. Then have them kneel on both knees. This is the "catching" position. The chair should be at one end of their "catch net."

Tell them: "It's important that you catch your friend who's going to make the plunge. You have to catch him/her. You cannot fail. There's no room for error. The person who is going to plunge is placing his/her life in your hands. You have to succeed."

Now talk to the students who will take the plunge. Stress the importance of following every instruction. Begin by building that person's trust in those who are going to trust in the catchers. For example, you could say, "You're going to fall backwards off of this chair. They (point to the eight catchers) are going to catch you. They will not drop you. You have to trust them. They are going to be careful, and they will succeed."

Then explain how to make the plunge. The key is to keep the body straight and rigid so the person's weight is equally distributed over all the eight catchers. Explain it in the following way: "Fall like you are going to fall backwards into a pool of water, only this is a little bit different. There are three things that you must do.

1. "Keep your body straight and rigid. If you sit down, you'll go through their hands and fall to the floor.

2. "Put your head back when you take the plunge. This will help keep your body straight. Do not tuck your chin into your chest. This tends to make you sit rather than fall backwards completely straight.

3. "Keep your hands and arms to your side. Grab the outside seams of your pants if it will help. Do not swing your arms out as you fall. You will hit one of the catchers in the head if you do so."

Review the technique until you are sure this person is confident in what they are going to do. If the person hesitates, build his/her trust in the catchers again and review the plunge technique. If necessary, count to three with them, "One, two, three, plunge." Do not push the student. This tends to startle the person. It is important that they do this themselves.

Afterwards, let students talk and laugh among themselves for a minute or two, then pull the group together. Use this activity to illustrate the partnership between missionaries and supporters. The person who took the plunge represents the missionaries. The catchers represent the supporters here in the United States. In the same way as the person who took the plunge, missionaries plunge into missions depending on their supporters (represented by the catchers) to keep them from falling. Note the difference between "plunging" and "falling." A person plunges into something that he or she believes in and no one gets hurt. When a person falls, he/she gets hurt. Point out that at times supporters fail, but God never fails.

Below are some statistics that might help explain that Americans can still send and support more missionaries.

| | |
|---|---:|
| Foreign missionaries from the U.S. (All denominations) | 285,250 |
| Short-term foreign missionaries from the U.S. (All denominations) | 180,000 |
| Foreign mission boards or societies in the U.S. (All denominations) | 3,970 |
| Number of Christians in the U.S. (All denominations) | 200,000,000 |
| Number of Christian churches in the U.S. (All denominations) | 400,000 |
| Average number of foreign missionaries supported by one Christian church in the U.S. | 7 |
| Average number of Christians in the U.S. that support one missionary. | 701 |

Foreign missionary statistics—David B. Barrett and Todd M. Johnson, *Our Globe and How to Reach It: Seeing the World Evangelized by A.D. 2000 and Beyond* (Birmingham, Ala.: New Hope,1990).

Christians in the U.S. statistics—based on figures in David B. Barrett, ed., *World Christian Encyclopedia: A Comparative Survey of Churches and Religions in the Modern World, A.D. 1900–2000*. Nairobi: Oxford University Press,1982.

# Sharing the Gospel "Goodies"

"The harvest is plentiful, but the workers are few. . . ."(Luke 10:2)

Give each youth a piece of paper at the beginning of the meeting (32 percent receive green paper, 68 percent receive brown paper). During the meeting, students with the green paper receive candy and can get up and move around. They can eat their food, hold it, or share it with others. The people with the green paper represent those who know Christ and have received the "goodies" of the gospel. The people with brown paper represent non-Christians who have not yet received the gospel. This activity reinforces Christian young people's responsibility to share the gospel.

## When to Use

- Use during the preliminaries of a meeting to capture the students' attention for a message.

- Use at a retreat or a missions banquet.

## Objectives

To present an accurate picture of the percentage of the world's population who have not received Christ.

To cause young people to think of their responsibility to share the gospel.

To illustrate to young people the various "worlds" around them—school, neighborhood, community, country, and foreign countries—which include lost people, so that they will begin to share Christ now, where they are.

## Materials

☐ Pieces of paper two inches by two inches (approximate size), one per person. Thirty-two percent of the pieces should be green and sixty-eight percent brown.

☐ Variety of candy that can be eaten quickly and easily during the meeting.

☐ Soft drinks (if appropriate for your setting).

## Preparation

Cut up pieces of paper (green and brown) to give one per person. Mix the pieces of paper together and have them ready to hand out as students walk into the meeting.

Put candy in serving dishes and have soft drinks available.

## Method

Hand out the pieces of paper randomly. During the preliminaries of the meeting, periodically stop and have the students with green pieces of paper get up and get candy and soft drinks (or you may want to pass the items out instead). When the students have returned to their seats, they can eat the candy, put it in their pockets, or share it with their friends. After doing this several times, then those with the brown paper will be complaining to you about not having the same privileges. Respond by telling them to ask the students with green paper for candy and drinks.

At an appropriate time, call an end to the activity. You may want to pass out candy and drinks to all the young people to even the score. Then, ask those with brown paper, "What did you feel like when you were excluded from the food privileges? Did your friends share with you? What did you feel towards them? What would you like to do to those who did not share?"

Also ask those with green paper, "What did it feel like to have special food privileges? How did you handle it? Did you share? Did you withhold food? Did you tantalize and tease? Did you ignore?"

Explain that this has been a simulation of what's happening in the real world. Thirty-two percent of the world is Christian. They were represented by those people holding the green paper. Sixty-eight percent of the world is non-Christian. They were represented by those holding brown paper. The food represented the gospel. It is up to Christians to give the gospel to the non-Christian world. Emphasize that God wants to use them to reach the world. Emphasize all the various "worlds" around them such as their schools, neighborhoods, communities, country, and foreign countries.

The numbers and percentages below will help the young people grasp the vast multitude of people who do not know Christ.

This chart lists number of Christians as a percentage of each of their continent's total population.

| | Number of Christians | | Population of Continent | | Percentage of Christians | |
|---|---|---|---|---|---|---|
| | 1985 | 2000 | 1985 | 2000 | 1985 | 2000 |
| Africa | 236,278,850 | 393,326,210 | 520,381,640 | 813,390,700 | 45.4 | 48.4 |
| East Asia | 22,324,690 | 33,337,300 | 1,168,795,000 | 1,373,242,000 | 1.9 | 2.4 |
| Europe | 420,926,340 | 431,403,570 | 499,909,700 | 539,536,500 | 84.2 | 80.0 |
| Latin America | 392,204,600 | 571,157,820 | 419,181,775 | 619,934,100 | 93.6 | 92.1 |
| North America | 227,237,570 | 253,589,490 | 260,828,500 | 296,203,000 | 87.1 | 85.6 |
| Oceania | 21,537,492 | 27,741,966 | 25,657,360 | 32,714,700 | 83.9 | 84.8 |
| South Asia | 125,914,645 | 192,264,050 | 1,609,178,000 | 2,269,594,000 | 7.8 | 8.5 |
| USSR | 102,168,000 | 118,101,000 | 281,192,000 | 315,027,000 | 36.3 | 37.5 |
| Global Christianity | 1,548,592,187 | 2,019,921,366 | | | 32.3 | 32.2 |
| World Population | | | 4,781,123,975 | 6,259,642,000 | | |

Source: David B. Barrett, ed. *World Christian Encylopedia: A Comparative Survey of Churches and Religions in the Modern World, A.D. 1900–2000.* Nairobi: Oxford University Press, 1982, p.4, 782-785. (Contains a complete listing of adherents of all religions by continents.)

To figure the population or percent for any given year between 1985 and 2000, calculate the difference in population or percentage between 1985 and 2000. Divide by 15 and multiply by the number of years over 1985. Add that to the 1985 figures.

# PART II

# *Reflective Activities*

These activities provide opportunity for young people to contemplate and assimilate Christ's mandate on missions. They promote group discussion and help young people focus on the missions theme.

# Before and After

"But God demonstrates his own love for us in this: While we were still sinners, Christ died for us." (Romans 5:8)

Students make two drawings of a person of any nationality. The first sketch is of someone before he or she has accepted Christ. The second sketch is the same person after having accepted Christ. This helps students visualize the changes Christ makes in people.

## When to Use

- Use as the missions segment for a meeting.
- Use as an introduction to a message.
- Use as an illustration in a message.
- Use as a follow-up to a message.

## Objective

To help students visualize the changes Christ brings to a person's life, which enables students to understand the importance of missions and evangelism.

## Materials

- ☐ A sheet of 8 1/2" x 11" paper for each person.
- ☐ One pencil per student.

## Preparation

Gather materials and prepare workers for this activity. Explain to your workers ahead of time how you want to do the activity and its purpose. During the activity, workers can mingle among the group to encourage students and help them draw.

## Method

Pass out the paper and pencils. Ask students to think of a foreign national (Asian, European, Latin American, African, or Middle Easterner) who does not know Christ as Savior. Ask them to think about what the person would look like. Would he/she be happy or sad, excited or depressed, friendly or mean, etc.? How might that person dress, behave, speak, or what might they believe?

Then have the students fold their papers in half and draw this person on the top half of the paper. This will be their drawing of the person before they accept Christ and His ways.

Next, on the bottom half of the paper, have them draw the same person after he/she has accepted Christ. Have them note the differences. Discuss how Christ can make a difference in a person's life. Use this activity to challenge your young people for missions. Adapt it to apply to your situation.

This activity can be done individually or in small groups. If done in small groups, have a youth worker responsible for each group. When they have finished their drawings, have volunteers in each group stand, show, and explain their drawings to everyone. Use this format to comment about the differences and have a group discussion.

# Concerns and Excitements

"For he guards the course of the just and protects the way of his faithful ones." (Proverbs 2:8)

In this activity students list the things that would concern them and excite them if they were to live in a foreign country. It helps them relate to missionary kids and missionaries.

## When to Use

- As an introduction to a message.
- As a lead-in to a meeting.
- As a lead-in to prayer time.

## Objectives

To help young people focus on the practical aspects of missions so they can understand the challenges and concerns experienced by missionaries.

To cause young people to think about daily life as a missionary living overseas in order that they can empathize with the needs of missionaries and their children.

## Materials

☐ A sheet of paper or an index card for each student.

☐ One pencil per person.

☐ Preparation.

☐ Gather materials to prepare workers for this activity. Explain to your workers the purpose of the session and their responsibilities.

## Method

This activity can be done individually or in small groups. Have the students choose a country that they would like to live in, or assign countries to them. Have them list the things they would be concerned about or afraid of with regard to living in that country. Then have them list the things they would be excited about in that country.

Follow this with a time of discussion about what missionaries and their children face overseas. If you have a missionary family visiting the church, see if they have a teenage son or daughter who can share their impressions of being overseas.

Follow this up by challenging your students regarding missions. Ask how they would reach people with the gospel and how they would deal with their own concerns.

# Dear Youth... I Need Your Advice

"I can do everything through him who gives me strength." (Philippians 4:13)

This activity is similar to a "Dear Abby" column in the newspaper. Young people review letters from fictional missionary kids relating real-life problems actually faced by missionary kids. In each case, one missionary kid is seeking advice. The students respond by writing a "Dear Abby"-type of response letter. This activity is most effective when done in small groups and read to the entire group.

## When to Use

- Use to start a meeting.
- Use to introduce a message.
- Use as a lead-in to the concluding service.

## Objectives

To give students a glimpse of the different situations missionary kids find themselves having to deal with overseas, which will cause them to realize the difficulties of living in another country.

To challenge students to offer solutions for the problems faced by missionary kids, and then encourage them to apply their advice to their own life situations.

## Materials

☐ Paper and pencil for each small group.

## Preparation

Gather the materials needed. Copy the "Dear Youth" letters so each letter is on a separate piece of paper ready to hand to each group. Have students do this activity in small groups. Explain the activity to your workers. Instruct them to move from group to group helping with their responses. Plan for each group to read its letter to the entire group.

Plan a challenge to students regarding their advice. While they are reading their letters aloud to the entire group, you will hear various kinds of advice that could also be applied to their own stateside situations. Challenge students regarding missions and regarding their own lives.

Below are nine brief letters from teenage missionary kids to your students. The letters are fictional, but are based on true-life experiences of missionary kids.

Dear Youth,

I am going to boarding school for the first time, and although I'm excited about it, I'm a little bit worried about being away from home for nine months out of the year. The school is set up on trimesters, so I get to come home every three months, but that's still a long time to be away. Boarding school is 1,000 miles from home and in a different country. What can I do to get ready to make the most of my boarding school experience?

Ready, But Worried

Dear Youth,

The first thing I saw when I got off the plane was an anti-American march. People here really hate the United States. They don't like anything about us. They don't even like to speak English to me. I'm trying really hard to learn the language quickly, but they don't seem to notice and won't help. I don't know if I can take it for four years! I hate being hated. What can I do?

Hate Being Hated

Dear Youth,

I don't know if there are more than four Christians in this country; dad, mom, my brother, and myself . . . and I'm not absolutely sure about my brother. This place is hedonistic! The neighbors burn incense and sacrifice animals. The bus driver looks demon-possessed, and drives like it too. How can I tell these people about Christ when they hate Christians so much?

It Ain't Easy

Dear Youth,

And I thought that my hometown in the U.S. was boring. This place has nothing to do. There are no high-tech video games or teenage hang-outs. Most of the people look as poor as refugees in a refugee camp. The teenagers all work to earn money for their families. I feel like a millionaire in comparison. Part of me hurts for these people, the other part makes me thankful that at least I live in a nice home. How can I come to grips with my conflicting feelings?

Loving It and Hating It

Dear Youth,

The closest American is three islands away. Mom tries to keep me busy, but I still can't help remembering all the friends I had in the States. School starts in four weeks, and mom says there will be a lot of new friends for me there, but I still get lonely. Is there anything I can do to keep from getting so low?

Lonely Island

Dear Youth,

I'm scared! I know I've been to missionary kid boot camp and I can handle just about anything, but I'm still scared. You see, this country is at war with two other countries. It is common to have bomb threats, terrorist raids, and kidnappings around here. I'm not so worried about myself because we're living in an area away from the trouble, but my dad takes trips almost every day in areas where bombs go off. I am afraid for his life! I don't want him hurt. How can I be at peace with this situation?

Peace In War

Dear Youth,

My parents said, "Give it five months," and I'd be over the major cross-cultural adjustments. Well, I'm not! I still don't know the rules to the games. In fact, I don't even know half of the sports they play over here. And do you think anyone's willing to teach me? No, they just go off and play. Am I supposed to learn by osmosis? Why won't anyone learn football? I need help, and don't tell me the problem is with my attitude! My mom tells me that all the time.

Still In Culture Shock


Dear Youth,

I'm so frustrated at school! I have to wear a uniform, raise my hand before I speak, and ask permission in front of everyone just to go to the bathroom. I also have to use a ruler to underline my math problems, and I have to stand at attention when I speak. Today, I forgot and spoke without doing all of this and got into big trouble. The teacher yelled at me so loud that I think the principal could have heard it down at his office. This whole school system is so different than what I'm used to. How will I ever learn to function here?

Too Many School Rules


Dear Youth,

My parents have been itinerating for nine months. I switched over to correspondence school so I can travel with them. I like going along and traveling across the United States, but on the other hand I dislike feeling like I am on display in front of every church for every pastor. What is the best way to handle this?

On Display


## Method

Introduce this activity to your young people by asking how many of them have friends who live overseas. Comment that the average young person in America doesn't understand what a person would go through living in a foreign country. Explain that in this activity they will get a glimpse of some of the frustrations and challenges that missionary kids face.

Have the students form into small groups and have the workers pass out the letters from the MKs. Have each group designate a person to write the letter and a person who will read the letter to the large group at the end of the activity. Follow the activity with a challenge to pray for the missionary kids and to apply what they have learned to their own situations.

# Here and There

"No one who has left home or brothers or sisters or mother or father or children or fields for me and the gospel will fail to receive a hundred times as much. . . ." (Mark 10:29)

In this activity, students make a list of the people, places, and things they would like to take overseas with them if they were to move. Next, they list the things they could realistically take with them. Finally, they compare the two lists. This activity should help students understand the separation from American culture that missionaries and missionary kids experience, and it should help them discover a little bit about themselves.

## When to Use

- As an introduction to a message.
- As a lead-in to a prayer time.

## Objectives

To help students understand what missionaries and missionary kids leave behind when they move overseas so that they are better informed regarding cross-cultural adjustments.

To help students realize what is important to them so they can see how important Jesus Christ is to them.

## Materials

☐ A sheet of 8 1/2" x 11" paper for each person.
☐ A pencil for each person.

## Preparation

Gather materials and prepare workers for the activity. Explain the purpose to your workers and how you want them to help you. If you decide to do this activity in small groups, then assign one worker to each group.

## Method

Explain to the students that one of the biggest cross-cultural adjustments for missionaries and missionary kids is dealing with the separation from people, places, and things in the United States. Ask your students to think of what life would be like if suddenly there were no more McDonald's, malls, skateboards (or some other latest fad), VCRs, prime-time TV shows, Saturday morning cartoons, close friends, etc.

This activity can be done individually or in small groups. Have the students make two lists, filling out one list at a time. On the first list have them write down all the people, places, or things that they would like to take overseas with them if they were going to live there for four years. Their lists could include anything, such as a shopping mall, McDonald's restaurant, all their friends at school, and so on. These will be their wish list. When they have finished, have them make a second list of the things they can actually take over with them. This would narrow the list down to things they could take in a suitcase or could be shipped over on a boat. When everyone has finished, have them share their lists within their small groups, or the large group if you have done this activity individually.

Both of the lists contain items that are important to them. Challenge students about what place of importance Jesus Christ has in their life. Does He come in at top, middle, or bottom of these two lists? Would they be willing to give up things on their list to serve Christ? Also, you can ask them to prioritize their list. This will further identify the things of utmost importance in their lives.

This would be an excellent time to encourage students to cultivate good relationships with each other and with Christ. Have them look on their list to see how many people they have listed. Explain to them that these are the important people in their lives.

Close with prayer for your young people and prayer for missionary families.

# Missions Is...

"I have made you a light for the Gentiles, that you may bring salvation to the ends of the earth." (Acts 13:47)

Sentence completion is an excellent way for young people to express their ideas, thoughts, and feelings. Through this sentence completion activity, students can share their impressions about missions, the world, God, and themselves.

### When to Use

- Use as an introduction to a message.
- Use as a separate missions segment.
- Use on a missions retreat.

## Objective

To provide an opportunity for students to verbalize their ideas, thoughts, and feelings about missions. As a result they will learn more about missions and their desire for involvement.

## Materials

☐ Paper and pencil for each person or small group.

## Preparation

Gather materials for the activity. Choose the sentence starters that most apply to your students and the direction you want them to explore. Create your own sentences as needed.

Run through the activity with your workers. This will help you prepare for challenging students with the missions message, and it will help your workers be more effective in helping the students. Instruct your workers to mill among the students to help them with ideas. The following is a list of sentence starters.

If God called me to be a missionary, _____.

If I were a missionary kid, _____.

The world would be a better place if _____.

God feels _____ for the world.

I would like to help people in _____ (name of country).

I would like to help _____ (name of people group).

If I were God, missions _____.

People who don't know Christ _____.

The best thing about ministering overseas would be _____.

The toughest thing about ministering overseas would be _____.

Young people in the United States can help the missions effort by _____.

People in _____ (name of country) need _____.

Children around the world _____.

Teens around the world _____.

## Method

This activity can be done two different ways: individually, or in small groups. If you decide to use the individual method, give each young person several sentence starters and have them complete each one. If you choose to go with the small group method, give each group one sentence starter and have them complete it in four to six different ways.

At the end of the activity, have students share their sentences and additional comments with the entire group. Challenge students for missions and end in prayer.

# Missions Line Up

"Therefore, my dear brothers, stand firm. Let nothing move you. Always give yourselves fully to the work of the Lord. . . ."(1 Corinthians 15:58)

Students line up along a line (running the length of the room) according to how they feel regarding certain missions issues. The extreme positions on the ends of the line are "strongly agree" and "strongly disagree." Students line up anywhere along the line between those two extremes. The neutral area would be somewhere in the middle. This helps youth discover how they feel about missions issues and helps them make a public stand about their position.

## When to Use

- Use as an opener for a meeting.
- Use as an introduction to the missions topic/segment of a meeting.
- Use at the conclusion of a missions message.

## Objectives

To help students define missions-related issues to decide how they feel about those issues.

To bring students to an understanding of their feelings about missions-related issues that will encourage them to take a strong stand on those issues.

## Materials

☐ Paper and pencil for each person or small group (optional).

## Preparation

Make a single line down the length of the room with a roll of masking tape. In this activity, either yourself or a youth worker will read a statement regarding missions. Students will then line up along the line according to how they feel about that statement. Those who strongly agree will be on one end, while those who strongly disagree would stand at the other end. The rest would stand at various places in between those two extremes. You may find that with some issues students are evenly spread along the line, while on other issues they tend to cluster together. You also may find that some young people will have a hard time making up their minds.

There are three basic ways to discuss the issues:

1.   Have the students talk about why they chose the position (along the line) During this discussion, students can shift positions at any time. They may be persuaded by someone else's viewpoint.

2.   Students can write a brief sentence or two on why they believe the way they do about that issue. Then they can read their statements, or the statements can be gathered and anonymously read by a worker or other students.

3.   You can cluster students with similar viewpoints together for small group discussion, after which each group would report back to the entire group.

The following are suggested statements for this activity.

1.   Jesus is the only way to heaven and peace with God.

2.   Youth cannot do much in missions.

3.   Only missionaries are called to be witnesses.

4.   It is important for missionaries to learn the culture of the people to whom they are ministering.

5.   Other religions contain truth.

6.   Missionaries should feed hungry people and help suffering people before they talk to them about Christ.

7.   Missionaries must be called by God.

Include other questions that would be more pertinent to your students.

Explain the activity to your workers. Instruct them how you want them to assist. Often, it works best if the workers make their stand about issues along with the students.

General guidelines for the activity:

1.   Students should give reasons for why they have chosen a position.

2.   Students can shift positions at any time.

3.   It's okay for students to try to convince other individuals or groups to change their point of view.

## Method

Introduce the concept to the students. Explain how the activity works. Have everyone stand. Read a statement and have students go to the appropriate position along the line. When all students have stationed themselves, begin the discussion (according to the way you have chosen to do the activity: that is, one individual discussion, individually writing down reasons, or in small groups). At the end of the allotted time (or when the young people have concluded their discussion), move on to the next statement and repeat the activity.

Conclude this activity by challenging students regarding missions and specifically the issues you have discussed in the activity. End with prayer.

# Sculpturing the World

"Through him all things were made; without him nothing was made that has been made." (John 1:3)

Students use colorful wire pipe cleaners to sculpture shapes or symbols relating to world missions. This is effective as an opener for a discussion.

## When to Use

- Use to introduce the missions theme or segment of a meeting.
- Use as a lead-in to a message.
- Use as a lead-in to prayer time.
- Use at a missions retreat.

## Objective

To focus students' attention, through the use of sculpturing or symbols, on aspects of world missions, expanding their awareness of missions.

## Materials

☐ Wire pipe cleaners (purchased at a fabric or craft store or the fabric section of a department store). Provide up to four pipe cleaners per person, depending on your budget.

## Preparation

Decide what you want the young people to sculpture. It can be a shape or symbol of the missions theme, a burden, prayer request, something they've learned about a foreign country, something they like about a foreign country, a person or people group, and so on.

You may want to have students sculpture a particular theme that would coincide with your message, or simply ask them to sculpture anything about missions.

Do your own sculpture before the meeting to use as an example when you introduce the activity to the students. Run through the activity with your youth workers as a way to prepare them to help the students with ways to express their ideas.

This activity can be done individually or in small groups. In a small group, all members of the group would combine their wire and efforts to produce one sculpture.

### Method

Pass out the wire cleaners and introduce the activity. Use your own sculpture or one of your youth worker's sculptures as an example. When the students have finished with their sculptures, have them share the meaning or story behind what they've made. They can do this in their small groups or with the entire group, whichever works best.

# Trusted Friends

"May the Lord make your love increase and overflow for each other and for everyone else." (1 Thessalonians 3:12)

All of us have people we consider "trusted friends." These are the people closest to us emotionally, and with whom we feel comfortable sharing our thoughts and feelings. This activity helps young people identify the trusted friends in their lives, and will give them a certain understanding of the separation and loneliness missionaries and their children experience when they move overseas.

### When to Use

- Use as a lead-in to a message.
- Use as a challenge and lead-in to a prayer time.

### Objectives

To help students, by asking them to identify their most trusted friends, to understand and empathize with the difficulty that missionaries and their children face in separation from friends and family.

To help students recognize the need everyone has for friendship so they will be motivated to reach out to new young people moving into their community.

## Materials

☐ Hand out sheets—"My Trusted Friends," one per person.

☐ One pencil per person.

## Preparation

Fill out the "My Trusted Friends" sheet yourself. Note which names you list most frequently. These are your most trusted friends. How many are family members? Relatives? Work/school associates? Peers? If you were to move overseas, how many of these people would move with you? You would experience separation and loneliness from having to leave your friends. How would it feel to have to replace those friends? Many times missionaries and their children go through periods of grief with the separation from their friends.

Lead your staff through the exercise. This will help them prepare to help students when they do the exercise. Ask them to identify and reach out particularly to the young people who are lonely or seem to have no friends.

## Method

Pass out the "My Trusted Friends" sheet and have everyone fill it out individually. Lead students through the exercise. Follow it with a discussion about friendship and a challenge to your young people.

Optional: Ask students for which statements that they would put down a pet or stuffed animal's name. Perhaps some would have liked to have put down a friend, relative, family member who has recently died. Ask why it was easy to share their feelings and thoughts with those particular people or animals.

# MY TRUSTED FRIENDS

*Complete each sentence with the name of a person. You can use any person's name as many or as few times as you would like. All people you refer to must be alive.*

1. I can be adventurous with _____.

2. I can share my disappointments with _____.

3. It's okay for me to be angry with _____ (because we can work it out.)

4. I love to laugh with _____.

5. It's okay for me to cry with _____.

6. I can be ecstatic around _____.

7. I can really be myself with _____.

8. Someone I can talk to about an embarrassing experience is _____.

9. I can be quiet and comfortable with _____.

10. Someone I can talk to seriously about my dreams and hopes

    is_____.

11. I can go to _____ when I am really scared.

12. I can go to _____ when I have a major problem.

13. I can show affection with _____ (verbal and non-verbal affection).

14. Someone I can talk to easily about my problems is _____.

# What the World Needs

"The people living in darkness have seen a great light; on those living in the land of the shadow of death a light has dawned." (Matthew 4:16)

More and more, we hear of world events such as wars, coups, terrorism, famine, drought, volcanic eruptions, flooding, earthquakes, and so on. For a one- to two-week period, have students clip out news articles from newspapers and news magazines about these kinds of events occurring in foreign countries. These articles will become the focus of small group discussion and prayer.

## When to Use

- Use as an introduction to a meeting.
- Use as a lead-in to a message.
- Use as a lead-in to a prayer or commitment time.
- Use as an activity at a missions retreat.

## Objective

To increase students' awareness of world events and how these events affect people. As a result, students will learn about the needs of people and how they, as a group, can help to meet those needs.

## Materials

☐ Newspaper or news magazine clippings of various world events.

☐ Pencil and paper for each small group.

## Preparation

Plan to do this activity in small groups. Ask specific students to scan the international section of newspapers and news magazines, clipping out articles of world events. Have them look for events that:

1. Affect people in some way, either positively or negatively.

2. Occur in foreign countries.

For example: Spread of diseases, cure of diseases, death of leaders or prominent people, murders, assassinations, wars, political coups, terrorism, earthquakes, flooding, famine, drought, volcanic eruptions, good will on the part of certain people, feeding programs, education programs, job training programs, and so forth.

Pick out articles yourself to use in preparation to challenge the students. Have your youth workers search out articles too. This will help them prepare for the meeting. It will also give you back-up articles in case some of the kids forget to bring them.

Prepare a series of questions for the small groups to discuss such as:

1. What was the nature of the event? Briefly describe.

2. How did this event affect people/change their lives?

3. How do you think the people felt?

4. What do you think they need now?

5. How can we help?

## Method

Form students into small groups. Each group should have one news article. Introduce the activity by talking about world events and challenging students to think about what the Christian response should be to the particular situation that they will be reviewing.

Have each small group work through the series of questions (given above) and write down the group's responses. Then give time for each group to report back to the entire group. As time permits, allow for discussion, your message, and prayer. Challenge young people to a commitment to help through the local church, denominational programs, or para-church programs.

During prayer time, give thanks for the good things that have happened internationally. Also pray for the people who are struggling or suffering because of negative events.

# PART III

# *Cultural Awareness*

These activities help students develop a greater awareness of the various cultural systems in our world. They promote participation, increase learning, and help students focus on the missions message. These are effective as openers, setting the atmosphere for a meeting, and introducing a message.

# Cross-Cultural Communication

"Declare his glory among the nations, his marvelous deeds among all peoples." (Psalm 96:3)

This simulated activity demonstrates what it is like to try to speak to someone who does not understand your language. When people travel to countries where they do not understand the language, they are forced to try to communicate without speaking. This activity lets students feel what that is like. This activity can be for a group from 10 to 100.

## When to Use

The following are some options on how to use this activity.

- Use it as an introduction to a missions service to get the young people involved.
- Use it to introduce a message.
- Use it at a missions retreat.
- Use it to train young people before traveling overseas on a short-term missions trip.

## Objective

To present students with a culture shock experience so they can realize the communication difficulty missionaries and their children face when they arrive in a country where people speak another language.

## Materials

☐ None.

## Method

Explain that everyone should make a single line around or along the room, according to their birthdays (for example, January 10, January 14, March 23, June 1 . . . December 29). Age order is not important. They should decide which end of the line will be January, and which will be December. There is one important rule, however; no one can talk during this activity—no communication with their mouths, no whispering or mouthing the words. They may ask questions ahead of time like, "Can we use hand signals?" "Can we write?" Respond by simply stating, "You cannot use your mouth."

Make sure everyone gets the idea. Give the signal, "Go." As the leader, you can join in also. Watch the various students' reactions. Some will be frustrated or confused. You may need to remind them, "No talking." Remember: any communication is all right except using their mouths. They will quickly figure out that using hand signals/signing is the most effective way to communicate. They may also write or show birthdays printed on drivers licenses.

When everyone is in place, call the activity to an end by shouting, "Stop." Have them stay where they are. Ask if everyone has found their places? If not, help people find the right places, assuring them that they need not feel embarrassed. Use this as an opportunity to show the rest of the group how adjusting to a new culture and language can be embarrassing and confusing. You can say something like, "John has experienced what most people experience when they arrive in a new country. It is hard to figure out how to communicate with those people." Then turn to John and ask, "How does it make you feel?" Encourage him to be honest. If he does not say much, ask him, "Did you feel foolish, frustrated, embarrassed?"

Have the students say their birthdays in order. This way you can spot anyone who might be out of order. Help him or her find the right place. Again, use this opportunity to teach others and to ease the embarrassment for the participants.

Now lead into a brief discussion by asking the students how they felt while doing this activity. You may get comments about feeling frustrated, confused, fun, something new, etc. You may want to go on and state the observations that you made, along with some of the following questions: "How did you communicate?" "Did you notice anyone cheating or talking?" Point out that in a foreign country you may want to "cheat," but you can't because you don't know the language. Ask, "Why do you think some of you cheated?" Answers may include that students wanted to fit in quickly or that they didn't want to be embarrassed, etc. Explain that these are all normal feelings. If any of the students have traveled overseas, encourage them to comment about their experiences on first arriving in a foreign country.

# Culture Night

"Those who had been scattered preached the word wherever they went." (Acts 8:4)

Ahead of time, youth leaders create a culture for the meeting. The meeting room becomes a "country" where students must do as the culture dictates. This activity involves all the senses in helping young people learn about missions in an exciting way.

## When to Use

- Use to open a meeting.
- Use for a missions event or retreat.
- Use as part of training for a missions work day or a missions trip.

## Objectives

To transport students into another culture so that they may learn the differences in customs that exist from country to country.

To confront students with specific cultural differences and their importance in order that they may understand the transition experienced by missionaries and their children when they go overseas.

## Materials

- ☐ Beef stew to be eaten with fingers (enough for everyone to have two or three bites).
- ☐ Foreign decorations—pictures, costumes, art effects, posters (get from a travel agent).
- ☐ Foreign music (obtained at a library).
- ☐ Lots of napkins.
- ☐ A cultural symbol such as a name tag, dot, star, or face painting. This is to be worn on the forehead (or another place on the body that would not be customary for them such as cheek, arm, shoe, etc.).

## Preparation

At a previous meeting, announce that the next youth meeting will be culture night. The room will be transformed into a country with a national song, national food, and its own way of doing things.

Arrange the following:

1. Set up cultural rules: Rules can include some or all of the following:
   a. Bow and touch heads instead of using the hand shake or hugs as a greeting.
   b. Allow no physical contact except when greeting.
   c. Call all youth sponsors "chiefs."
   d. Call the youth pastor "chief chief."
   e. Don't allow girls to make eye contact with guys.
   f. Don't allow students to make eye contact with the "chiefs" or the

"chief chief" until the "chief"/"chief chief" has spoken to them.

g. In order to enter the culture, the students must agree to participate in all cultural activities—in other words, to abide by all cultural rules.

*Note: Youth sponsors will be the nationals of your new country. The students will be the guests in your country.*

2. Create a name and come up with a song for your new country. Your song can be an existing song or one that you have made up. Another option would be for your country to have a national rap rather than a song.

3. Set up a welcome area for the students. It should consist of:

   a. a place where the cultural rules are displayed on a huge sign for everyone to read as they enter.

   b. a place for students to take off their shoes and give them to a shoe caretaker.

   c. a table with food for the youth to taste and mingle over. There should be no silverware. Students must eat this food with their fingers.

4. Remove all chairs and have your meeting on the floor.

5. Have music playing as students enter.

6. Decorate in a foreign motif. Some of the easier motifs are:

   a. tropical motif—palm trees, nets, beach scenes, etc.

   b. a Muslim motif—veils, turbans, crescent moons and stars, etc.

   c. an oriental motif—Ninja-type symbols, umbrellas, and Japanese faces with the slanted eyes, etc.

7. Have the students wear something from your cultural motif. It could be the culture symbol that you have created, or you might want to add sunglasses, Hawaiian-type lei, friendship bracelets, etc. Choose something that is inexpensive yet memorable.

## Method

Have everything in place and the music going before anyone arrives.

As students come in, direct them to read the cultural rules. Explain to them about the culture and that they are guests. It is important for students not to offend the nationals in this particular culture. Then have them proceed to the place where they remove their shoes and check them with the shoe attendant.

Next, have the students touch, smell, and taste the food. Have your youth sponsors mill around with the students. As they do so, they should act offended or angered if a student breaks one of the cultural rules. For example, if a young person has talked to leaders without addressing them as chief or has made eye contact before the youth sponsor addressed them. At an appropriate time, teach students the national song or rap and have everyone do it together.

Gather students on the floor for the meeting. Begin with a discussion about the event. Ask them questions like: "How did it feel?" "What is different about this culture from what you are used to?" etc.

As an option for a message, use a biblical character who had to move to another culture other than the one he or she grew up in. For example, Joseph, Paul, or Esther.

# Greetings

"We are therefore Christ's ambassadors, as though God were making his appeal through us." (2 Corinthians 5:20)

There are hundreds of ways people around the world greet one another. Some of them are more common than others, like the Oriental bow, the Western handshake, and the popularized Native American, "How." In this activity, young people are shown several greetings from foreign cultures and are given the opportunity to give these greetings to one another.

## When to Use

- Use to begin a youth meeting.
- Use to focus on a missions message.
- Use as a missions awareness segment in a meeting.
- Use as part of an orientation for a missions trip or project.

## Objectives

To acquaint students with various greetings practiced by people of other cultures to build their cultural awareness.

To emphasize to young people how important it is for missionaries and their children to know and practice these greetings. As a result, they will learn that one of the important goals of missionaries and missionary kids is to show friendship and mutual respect to others.

## Materials

☐ None.

## Preparation

Acquaint yourself with the following greetings:

1. *The Oriental bow:* Stand facing your partner. Bow slowly to about a 45 degree angle, keeping hands behind your back. Keep eye contact as you bow. This greeting shows mutual respect and courtesy. (Note how it is different for a servant who bows to a master. The master is not required to return the bow to the servant. This shows superiority over the servant instead of mutual respect).

2. *The two-handed handshake:* Stand facing your partner. Reach out with your right hand to shake hands as we do in the Western world. Then both people reach out with their left hands and clasp the back of the other person's right hand. This is done among some African cultures and shows a special warmth and welcome to each other.

3. *The double hug:* This hug is done first to the right and then to the left, as in the French culture. (Note that this greeting is done differently for girls than it is for guys. The guys throw their arms around each other's shoulders and slap each other on the backs. The girls place their hands on each other's shoulders and then lean forward to touch cheeks very lightly. For guy/girl hugs, the girl's hug pattern is followed. Both people keep their hands on the other person's shoulders, then touch cheeks lightly. Some people may make the appearance of touching cheeks without actually doing so.)

4. *The hand clap:* Some tribal cultures don't touch when they greet one another. Instead, they clap hands twice, pause, then clap twice more. As they do so, they give a verbal greeting with each pair of claps. For this greeting, partners should face each other and give the double clap greeting while saying "Tomala" (hello). This is a sign of friendship because the hands of both are empty—that is, neither have weapons in them.

## Method

There are several ways to do this activity depending on the setting and the size of your youth group.

1. For large groups: Have students find partners to do all the greetings with. Have them pair up with a person next to them or near them. You can have them choose someone they don't know or make choices based on color of eyes, schools attended, birthdays, and so on.

2. For any size group with extra time: Have students form into small groups and greet everyone in the group.

3. For medium-size to small groups: Have the students form two equal lines facing each other. Each person greets the person opposite him or her. Once everyone has completed the first greeting, have them take one step to the right. This shifts the two lines in opposite directions, putting each person in front of a new partner. The person on the end of each line (who will not have anyone in front of them at this point) should step across to join the end of the other line. Repeat this process until each person has done each greeting with five to ten people. Then introduce a new greeting and have them greet another five to ten people.

At the end, have students take their seats, then talk about how, as Christians, one of our goals is to show friendship and mutual respect to others. We do not go with weapons in our hands or demanding servitude.

# Hands On

"God was reconciling the world to himself in Christ, not counting men's sins against them." (2 Corinthians 5:19)

Dried food, curios, artifacts, and clothing from foreign countries are passed around to members of the group. Students examine these by looking at, smelling, touching, and tasting (when appropriate). This will spark their interest and awareness of differences in food and taste.

## When to Use

- Use as an attention-grabber before a message.
- Use as a foreign awareness segment at or near the beginning of a service.
- Use to illustrate a message (for example, if you're going to talk on clothing yourself with righteousness).

## Objectives

To expose young people to items from foreign cultures which will help them learn some of the differences between cultures.

To help students realize that God's love for people does not depend upon what they eat or wear, but upon the condition of their hearts.

## Materials

☐ Use the resources in your community such as travel agencies, libraries, museums (some loan out artifacts), foreign restaurants, foreign stores (e.g., Oriental food and gift stores), and some grocery stores (the deli section will sometimes order exotic foods for you). Also contact people in the community or congregation who have traveled. If you have timed this activity for when a missionary will be visiting your church, ask him or her, in advance, to bring artifacts. You may get ideas from him about the kind of food people in his part of the world eat. Stay away from messy foods.

- Below is a list of items from foreign countries that would create interest and would be fun:

    1. Dried foods—especially dried fish. It has a strong smell and usually comes with eyes, fins, and scales intact. (This is not for eating—for looking, touching, and smelling only.)

       Dried seaweed.

       Dried snacks such as squid snacks, and cuttlefish with flavored crackers. Ask at the Oriental food stores or other foreign food stores what would have a strong fish smell.

    2. Clothing—hats, scarves, dresses, skirts, knee-length shorts, and jackets. Make them available for young people to try on. It may be best to choose volunteers to try these on in front of the entire group.

    3. Materials/artifacts—wood carvings, metal figures, glass figurines, animal skins, utensils, knives, spears, shields, toys, etc.

    4. Musical instruments—a variety of guitars, xylophones, primitive flutes, drums, etc.

- Note: If you are in an area with very little foreign culture, then you will have to improvise. Here are some suggestions.

    1. Use a scarf to wrap around the neck and over the head of a girl or a guy, as they do in Muslim countries.

    2. Find various hats, such as a beret or straw hats, such as are used in Latin America.

    3. Find or make sandals. Some African cultures make sandals out of tires. They will cut tire tread to the shape of the foot and put one strap over the toes and another over the heel.

    4. Make a "sari" like the women wear in India. This is basically a piece of cloth that is 6 to 12 yards long wrapped around the whole body.

    5. Take a sheet, fold it in half, cut a hole, and use it as a robe, as they do in some desert countries.

    6. Make some strips of cloth and wrap it around someone's head to create a turban, like they wear in some Indian countries.

7. Use a dish towel and a rope. Put the dish towel on someone's head with the length of it flowing down over the back and sides of his head. Use the rope (or belt) around the head to hold the dish cloth down. This will resemble the Arab head coverings.

8. Fold a blanket in half, cut a hole in the middle, and put it over someone's head and shoulders (so the head comes through the hole) and this will resemble a poncho used in Latin American cultures.

- If you are having problems finding food, check with the deli and international food departments of the grocery store. Also, contact missionaries for ideas.

## Preparation

Find the items for this activity. Set up a security system—some students may want to take certain items home without asking.

## Method

Pass these items around for examination. One of the easiest ways would be to pass them out as you would distribute communion, using youth sponsors or students as ushers. In addition, you may want to put some items on display before or after the meeting. A note of caution: to protect the clothing from being mishandled, you may want to have two or three students come forward before the meeting and try the clothes on in kind of a fashion re-make style. Do this instead of allowing students to try on clothes randomly.

At the end of this activity, talk to young people about the condition of their hearts. Explain that it's not what a person wears on the outside or what he or she eats that counts. It's what is on the inside that counts. Some of the things that they examined during the meeting may cause them to want to reject people from those cultures. However, God accepts all people no matter what they eat or wear.

Another approach would be to talk to students about clothing themselves in righteousness.

# Missions Trip Simulation

"Do everything in love." (1 Corinthians 16:14)

Young people spend a day traveling and living in a simulated foreign country. They must carry passports, obtain visas, experience immigrations and border crossings, obey cultural rules, and barter for strange food which they then eat with their hands.

## When to Use

- Use in connection with a missions convention.
- Use to emphasize a youth missions program.
- Use as part of a missions retreat or orientation.

## Objectives

To provide an opportunity for young people to experience all aspects of a missions trip, through simulation, so that they can identify with what it's like to travel to a foreign country.

To expose students to new customs and cultures. As a result, they will recognize the importance of having flexibility when encountering new situations.

## Materials

☐ 1. A place to be the simulated foreign country. A farm works well.

☐ 2. Transportation from the church to the country—a bus or van.

☐ 3. Food that will fit in with the culture. It needs to be finger food such as sandwiches, meats, fruits, etc.

☐ 4. Travel documents, such as applications for passports, applications for visas, passports, travel tickets (see samples at end of lesson).

☐ 5. Money from the "foreign culture" (see sample at end of lesson).

☐ 6. Travel itinerary with handouts explaining the cultural rules, barter system, key words for the foreign culture, immigrations procedures, etc.

## Preparation

1. Choose a location for your simulated foreign country. A barn or wooded area on a farm works well.

2. Decide on a name for your country (see samples).

3. Create cultural rules (see samples).

4. Print applications for passports, applications for visas, passports, travel tickets and other handouts about customs and regulations in the culture.

5. Choose the kind of transportation you would like to simulate. A bus or a van can be used to simulate ground travel or air travel. If you decide to simulate ground travel, make plans for mechanical breakdowns along the

way. If you decide to simulate air travel, make plans to have a stewardess with in-flight safety procedures and snacks.

6. Choose staff members to be immigration officials, bus drivers/airline pilots, stewardesses, food stand owners, and citizens of the simulated country.

7. Figure the cost per person and build it into the passport application fee, visa application fee, and ticket price.

## Method

Plan this as an all-day event. Two weeks ahead of time, set up an "American Embassy" in your meeting place, complete with desk, American flag, and other official-looking things such as an American presidential seal, a picture of the President or Governor, etc. This will be where students sign up and pay for the event by filling out the applications for their passport and visas and paying the fees. The staff behind the desk should remain stern-looking and very businesslike.

Also set up a travel agency, complete with desk and travel posters from around the world. At this desk, students must purchase their travel tickets.

On the day of the event, as the students arrive, have them pick up their passports, visas, and tickets. Those who have not applied for these travel documents can do so at that time—however, the prices will be higher.

Gather the group together to give explanations about the event, cultural rules, purpose, etc. Explain that, though this is just a simulation, it will generate some real feelings and real emotions that missionary kids and missionaries have when they travel to foreign countries. This will give the young people a "feel" of what it is like to travel overseas. Distribute the handouts about customs and cultural rules as you talk about them (see samples).

Have a stern-looking immigration official checking passports, visas, and tickets as students leave the room to board the bus. No one can board the bus without a passport, visa, and a round-trip ticket.

If you decide to simulate bus travel in a foreign country, try stopping because of a "mechanical breakdown" near a convenience store and allow kids to get out and purchase some snacks while the bus is being "fixed." In this case, stop the bus a block or two from the convenience store so students will have to walk as they do so often in foreign countries.

If you decide to simulate air travel, have a stewardess greet each person and check tickets as they board. Before leaving, the stewardess should give the airline safety speech (you may need to provide a small battery-powered megaphone). The speech can go something like this:

"Thank you for choosing MuKappa World Airlines. Please fasten your seat belts, make sure your seats are in the upright position and your tray tables fastened to the seat in front of you. Your carry-on baggage should be placed in the compartments above your head or under the seat in front of you. By government regulation, this is a non-smoking flight. In the event of an emergency, the oxygen masks will come down from the ceiling. Place one over your nose and mouth and breath normally. When the captain receives clearance from the tower, he will taxi to the runway for takeoff. And again, thank you for choosing MuKappa World Airlines."

After this, the pilot may announce your departure: "Welcome aboard. This is Captain Mobeto. I now have clearance to taxi to the runway for take off. Today we will be flying at 30,000 feet above sea level. Now just sit back, relax, and enjoy the flight."

On the trip, the stewardess can hand out snacks—peanuts and soft drinks, then collect the empty wrappers and pop cans. The pilot can make periodic announcements about elevation level, air turbulence, and special sites of interest along the way.

When you arrive at the "foreign country," remind the students of customs and immigration procedures and key words for that culture, and emphasize the importance of not offending the citizens of that country. Politeness is the rule, no matter how difficult or inconvenient it may be. Instruct your immigration officials to detain a few of the students. Have a special place for them to stand and wait until everyone has gone through the customs and immigration procedure, and then bring these detainees through. This will simulate the hours of waiting that it takes to get through long lines in some countries.

For the remainder of the morning, gather the students for a service. Have a missionary speak about missions and how young people can be involved. You may want to promote some of the youth missions programs available. (Option: If you live near an airport, sometimes it is possible to obtain permission to take students through the security check to the departure gate and have a missionary speak to the group there.)

For lunch time, have the store owners provide the meal. Remind the young people of the barter system—that the prices are not fixed and may fluctuate, and that they can only purchase food by using the trade language (signing the price they're willing to give for the food with their fingers). As you observe the purchase of food, it should be done in complete silence.

After lunch, divide the large group into smaller groups for some interaction and sharing of feelings and thoughts about the simulation so far. Ask students how it felt to go through immigrations. How did it feel to have to barter for your food? Ask them what they imagine missionaries go through in trying to get used to a culture overseas. If you have anyone who has traveled abroad, have them share some of their experiences and feelings. You may also want to do some of the other missions activities listed in this book.

Depending on how students are feeling when it is time to leave, you may want to load the students back onto the bus without setting up immigrations and simply end the simulation.

# Application for Passport

1. Name _____
         *(First)*            *(Middle)*          *(Last)*

2. Address _____ Phone _____

3. Sex — M  F  *(circle one)*    4. Place of birth _____

5. Height _____    6. Color of hair _____    7. Color of eyes _____

8. Father's name _____    Birth place _____
      Birth date _____    U.S. citizen ☐ Yes  ☐ No

9. Mother's maiden name _____    Birth place _____
      Birth date _____    U.S. citizen ☐ Yes  ☐ No

PHOTO

*(Prayer card appoved, circle yourself)*

*If no photo, draw a picture of yourself*

10. In case of emergency, notify:

   _____

Address _____

   _____

   _____

Phone _____

11. Applicant's identifying documents
      ☐ School card  ☐ Library card
      ☐ Meal card    ☐ Other

12. _____
             (Signature)

OFFICIAL USE ONLY

| | |
|---|---|
| Fee _____ | Paid_____ |
| Approved _____ | Unapproved _____ |
| Agent _____ | Date _____ |

```
┌─────────────────────────────────────┐
│        APPLICATION FOR A            │
│  _____ VISA            │
│        (Name of Country)            │
└─────────────────────────────────────┘
```

1. Name   Mr.  Mrs.  Ms. _____
      *(circle one)*

2. Place of birth _____

3. Date of birth _____

4. Nationality _____

5. Address in U.S.A. _____

   _____

6. Occupation _____

7. Telephone _____

8. Passport No. _____

9. Nature of passport *(check one)*

   ☐ Regular          ☐ Official

   ☐ Diplomatic       ☐ Laissez Passer

┌─────────────────────────┐
│         PHOTO           │
│                         │
│  *(Prayer card appoved, │
│   circle yourself)*     │
│                         │
│  *If no photo, draw a   │
│   picture of yourself*  │
│                         │
└─────────────────────────┘

10. Place passport was issued _____ Date: _____

11. Valid until _____

12. Destination _____

13. Kind of visa requested *(check)*

    ☐ Single entry  ☐ Multiple entries  ☐ Transit  ☐ Stay: ___ days/ ___ months

14. Reason for visit *(check)*

    ☐ Tourism  ☐ Transit  ☐ Business  ☐ Conference  ☐ Family/Friends  ☐ Other

15. Address while in the country _____

16. Arrival date _____ from _____

17. Departure date _____ to _____

OFFICIAL USE ONLY

┌──────────────────────────────────┐
│ Fee _____  Paid_____ │
│                                  │
│ Approved _____ Unapproved _____│      _____
│                                  │
│ Agent _____ Date _____  │              *(Signature)*
└──────────────────────────────────┘

```
```

## Passenger ticket and baggage check

| Carrier Name | Date of Issue |
|---|---|
| Passenger Name (Not transferable) | |

| Travel Information | Official National Carrier–Mukappa World Shuttle (MKWS)<br>Class–1st, 2nd, Economy, or No class.<br>Status–Priority, MK Travel Club, Standby, Paying.<br>Meal–Yes or No depending on travel times. | | | | | | |
|---|---|---|---|---|---|---|---|
| From | Carrier | Number | Class | Date | Time | Status | Meal |
| To | | | | | | | |
| To | | | | | | | |
| To | | | | | | | |

| Fare in U.S. Currency | Fare in Foreign Currency | Passenger Signature |
|---|---|---|
| Agent | Representing | |

---

## Passenger ticket and baggage check

Conditions subject to change

| Carrier Name | Date of Issue |
|---|---|
| Passenger Name (Not transferable) | |

| Travel Information | Official National Carrier–Mukappa World Shuttle (MKWS)<br>Class–1st, 2nd, Economy, or No class.<br>Status–Priority, MK Travel Club, Standby, Paying.<br>Meal–Yes or No depending on travel times. | | | | | | |
|---|---|---|---|---|---|---|---|
| From | Carrier | Number | Class | Date | Time | Status | Meal |
| To | | | | | | | |
| To | | | | | | | |
| To | | | | | | | |

| Fare in U.S. Currency | Fare in Foreign Currency | Passenger Signature |
|---|---|---|
| Agent | Representing | |

# PASSPORT

United States
of America

---

UNITED STATES
OF AMERICA

Passport No. _____
Surname _____
Given Names _____
Nationality _____
Date of Birth _____
Place of Birth _____
Date of Issue _____
Place of Issue _____
Date of Expiration _____

PHOTO

(Prayer card
approved,
circle yourself)

If no photo,
draw a picture of
yourself

---

## V I S A S

DEPARTURES
This certifies that _____
(name)

_____ is allowed to depart

_____. Date _____
(place)

Official's signature:
_____

ENTRIES
This certifies that _____
(name)

_____ is allowed to enter

_____. Date _____
(place)

Official's signature:
_____

---

## V I S A S

DEPARTURES
This certifies that _____
(name)

_____ is allowed to depart

_____. Date _____
(place)

Official's signature:
_____

ENTRIES
This certifies that _____
(name)

_____ is allowed to enter

_____. Date _____
(place)

Official's signature:
_____

---

# Youth Missions Encounter Trip
*(Sample Handouts)*

Welcome! You are about to experience a whole new way of living. Today you will go "international." You will experience what missionaries and missionary kids (MKs) experience. You will visit the remote country of MuKappa (Greek letters for MK). You already have your passports, visas, and travel tickets. If your travel documents are in order, you will board the official MuKappa world shuttle for departure.

## Cross-Cultural Guidelines

Before you can make a successful international trip, there are some things you need to know. Following these guidelines will enhance your overseas experience.

1. Attitude is important. Keep an open mind. Be flexible, positive, creative, and approach this as an adventure.

2. Do not offend the citizens of the MuKappian culture. You can offend them by not being sensitive to the customs of their culture. Here are some helpful guidelines to follow.

   a. Try everything: their food, their language, and their customs.

   b. Do not do things that they find offensive, like whispering.

   c. Never put them down or put down anything about their culture.

   d. Smile even though you think that some of their customs are stupid and even though their food may taste terrible.

## MuKappian Customs
*by Kenny Earl*

**Greeting:**
When someone reaches toward you as if to shake your hand, place your hand on his or her shoulder and say "Yo." He will then withdraw his hand and be pleased that you returned his greeting. If you clasp his hand and shake it, then you are challenging his grandmother to a best-out-of-three mud wrestling match, and you are subject to arrest.

Do not make eye contact with a MuKappian until the MuKappian has spoken to you. If you speak to him first, you must look at the ground until he has addressed you.

Address all MuKappians as "chief" each time you speak to them.

**Eating:**
Do not drink before you are completely finished eating your food. Eat everything that is given to you to eat. Only use your left hand for eating and drinking. There are no utensils in MuKappa.

**Warnings:**
Whispering is very offensive to MuKappians.
Men and women should never touch in public.
Only use the trade language when negotiating and bartering.

**Trade language:**
All bartering and negotiating of purchase prices must be done in the MuKappian trade language, which is a form of sign language. Hold up one finger for one Megadough, two fingers for two Megadough, and so forth. If you speak during the bartering process, the purchase is immediately canceled.

**MuKappian Facts**
Money: The basic unit is "Megadough" (equivalent to one American dollar).
Population: 12 (last year's census).
Religion: Animism and worship of ancestors.

**MuKappian Language Sheet**
The following list of words and phrases will be essential for you to master as you prepare to communicate with the people of MuKappa.

**Money**
Megadough = one American dollar
Megamegadough = two American dollars
(and so forth)

**Greeting**
Yo = hello
(Notice: never say "hi" to a MuKappian. "Hi" means "I wish to arm wrestle your grandmother." Since the people of MuKappa are very peaceful, any public mention of violence or anger is a criminal offense and subjects the speaker to arrest.)

**Key words for customs and immigrations**
Visa rite? = "Did you lie on your visa form?"
Visa rong? = "Did you tell the truth on your visa form?"
Nobo = "Yes"
Yebo = "No"

**General conversation**
Namo Yamo? = "What is your name?"
Yamo + (name) = "My name is _____"
Yamo Namo? = "Who have you punched lately?"
Namo + (name) = "I'd like to punch _____"
Mickeybighand? = "What time is it?"
*(Note: You should answer the question "Mickeybighand?" by using your arms like the hands of the clock to show what time it is.)*
Gottapotty? = "Do you have a restroom around here?"

# People of the World

"Open your eyes and look at the fields! They are ripe for harvest." (John 4:35)

The planet's population is headed towards 6 billion people. The people of the world live in over 200 countries, speak as many as 12,000 different languages, and represent up to 24,000 people groups.[2] 9,100 languages have no Scripture.[3]

Collectively, the world's population practices or believes in 30,000 various religions. 66.8 percent of the world is non-Christian, 33.2 percent is Christian.

Every people group and country faces tremendous problems, from the need for salvation to the need for food. This small group discussion activity will direct the students to develop plans for helping meet those needs. The goal is to move the young people to prayer and action.

## When to Use

- Use as an introduction to a message.
- Use as a follow-up to a message.
- Use as a missions segment.
- Use for a prayer time.

## Objectives

To help young people discover world needs so that they may recognize the magnitude of those needs.

To challenge students to think of ways to meet world needs that will motivate them to set personal priorities for their own participation.

## Materials

☐ 4" x 6" index cards. Have enough cards to pass one card to each small group.

The following books will give excellent resource information:

☐ Patrick Johnstone, *Operation World: A Day-to-Day Guide to Praying for the World*, 4th ed. (England: Send-the-Light and WEC Publications, 1986).

☐ David B. Barrett and Todd M. Johnson, *Our Globe and How to Reach It: Seeing the World Evangelized by A.D. 2000 and Beyond* (Birmingham, Ala.: New Hope, 1990).

☐ Frank Kaleb Jansen, ed., *Target Earth: The Necessity of Diversity in a Holistic Perspective on World Mission* (Pasadena, California: University of the Nations/Hawaii and Global Mapping International, 1989).

## Preparation

Prepare 4″ x 6″ index cards with information regarding the areas you will cover during the missions emphasis section of your meeting. List the needs, people involved, geographic location, populations, percentages, and other appropriate information. Use the books listed above to find information. Following is a suggested list of topics:

Countries without an adequate witness

Languages without Scriptures

Religions of the world/non-Christian people groups

Megacities of the world and their problems

World hunger, famine

Medical relief, AIDS, and other diseases

World starvation/hunger

Suffering from war, earthquakes, and other catastrophes

## Method

Form small groups. Give each group an index card with the various needs listed on it. Have each group develop plans on how to provide for or reach those people. Ask them, "If you had a million dollars and a 50-person organization, how would you help?"

After five minutes (or less) have the groups choose a spokesperson and report their plans to the entire group.

Optional: Have each small group prepare a one paragraph prayer for the people on their index card. Have one person write down the prayer word for word. Then have each group read the prayer aloud in unison.

Challenge students to do what they can to help. Emphasize the importance of prayer and action. Have them consider future missions work (either temporary or career).

# Smelling Ministry

"Let your gentleness be evident to all." (Philippians 4:5)

Many cultures have odors which Westerners find offensive. In some cultures, people do not wear deodorant. In tropical areas when people meet together and there is no air conditioning, odors can get very strong. Marketplaces have no refrigeration, so meat and fish that are on display begin smelling. Spicy foods can have very pungent smells. In some areas, there are open sewers and stagnant pools of water that give off horrible odors. Through this activity, young people learn to handle a smelly situation without offending those of the host culture.

## When to Use

- At an indoor meeting, at the end of a missions emphasis.
- To introduce a missions emphasis in an outdoor meeting.
- At a retreat setting during a meal.

## Objectives

To give students firsthand experience in dealing with strong odors which often exist in other countries. This activity will increase their awareness of cultural differences.

To teach students how to respond appropriately to these smells in order not to offend the people of the host culture. The young people will learn that even a missionary's or missionary kid's response to smells can be viewed as a ministry.

## Materials

☐ Skunk scent (can be purchased at sporting goods stores).

☐ Candy or cookies (optional).

## Preparation

Purchase the skunk scent in quantities that will allow one drop per person. Before the service, assign and instruct workers to distribute the scent at the appropriate time during the meeting.

## Method

Before starting this activity, talk to the students about linking our concept of ministry to our reaction to offensive smells. In American youth culture, it is sometimes viewed as humorous to plug your nose and make a strange face at offensive odors. However, in some overseas cultures, and in certain settings, this kind of reaction would offend people. In turn, they might view Americans as offensive and carry that idea to their view of God. Make the application about the importance of witnessing through Christian behavior.

Tell students that they are going to experience a "smelling ministry" situation. There are certain guidelines for this activity. (1) They cannot stick their tongue out, plug their noses, make strange faces or horrible sounds at the smell. They must keep a "Christian" face, which is one that smiles. (2) When they receive the skunk scent they are to put their hands down at their sides until everyone has the scent.

Have your workers distribute the skunk scent by putting one drop on the back of the right hand of each kid. If you choose to hand out a snack with the scent, instruct the kids that they must eat the snack with their right hand. This way the student is faced with the dilemma of a desirable snack and an undesirable scent.

While students are doing this activity, remind them that they are not to show any signs that this scent offends their sense of smell. They can laugh and talk, but no offensive sounds, expressions, or gestures. (It may be good to do this activity at the end of the meeting, since the skunk scent does not wash off easily.)

# Touchy Feely

"It has always been my ambition to preach the gospel where Christ was not known" (Romans 15:20).

In some remote cultures, the appearance of foreigners is a rarity. Curious children come up to foreigners to touch them, pinch them, pull on their clothes, or pull on their hair. This is their way of testing to see if a foreigner is a real person. Through this activity, young people experience what it is like to be the center of attraction for these curious foreign children.

## When to Use

- Use this activity to begin a service.
- Use this activity to introduce a missions message or theme for a meeting.
- Use this activity as a mission message itself, encouraging the students to be sensitive to other people's behaviors.

## Objectives

To show young people how some people in remote cultures respond to seeing a foreigner for the first time. As a result, students will better understand the remoteness of some cultures and the challenges that missionaries and their children face in these situations.

To challenge students to offer suggestions on how they, as Christians, should respond to these people. Their participation will help them be more sensitive to other people's behaviors.

## Materials

☐ None.

## Preparation

Explain to your helpers or staff how children in some remote cultures would respond to a foreigner walking into their village. In this activity, they will simulate that situation. Children of a foreign culture would pinch, pull, and prod out of curiosity. In some cultures, long blonde hair would look like spider webs to them. Clothing might look like woven animal hair. They might not know what to make of bright-colored cloth. They would pinch light-colored skin to see if it felt the same as their own.

The key to success with this activity is to prepare helpers or staff ahead of time. Your staff will play the role of the foreigners who are curious about the Americans, who will be played by your students. During this activity, your staff should not speak any English. They can speak gibberish or, if they know a foreign language, have them speak it. They should pull on the students' hair, pinch their skin lightly, pull on their clothing, try to take things out of their pockets, try to take their watches off their wrists, take a shoe off someone's foot, take a hat, see if they can talk a student into removing a necklace or earring, and take glasses if some students are wearing them.

This activity works best if several staff converge on one student. Do not tell the young people ahead of time what is going to happen. The element of surprise enhances this activity. At the end of the activity, have a time of debriefing and explanation.

## Method

Have the students stand outside the door to your meeting room. Begin the activity by choosing one person to enter the room. Keep the rest outside so they cannot see what is going on. As soon as the first student enters the room, have your staff converge and begin the touchy-feely activity. Choose a time limit, such as one minute, for each young person to endure this experience. When the time limit is up, have one staff member speak to the student in English and direct him or her to a chair to watch the next student coming in for the same experience. Repeat this until all the students have undergone this experience.

For large groups, divide your staff so that you can bring in several students at one time and have them go through the activity simultaneously. After everyone has had a turn, ask them questions about their feelings during the experience. For example,

"How did you feel when the staff started to pinch your skin, pull on your hair, etc."

"What did you think was happening?"

"How did you want to respond?"

"How many of you got irritated?"

"How many thought this was fun?"

"How did you feel when no one would speak English?"

"Do you think this kind of thing actually happens anywhere in the world?"

After getting feedback from students, tell them why you have chosen this activity. Explain how curious children react to seeing a foreigner: that they are simply testing to see if the person is real; in some cultures blonde hair would look like spider webs to the children; to children who have dark skin, white skin is almost unbelievable—they want to touch it to see if it feels the same; in some cultures, children have no hair on their arms, so they might pull the hair on a foreigner's arms.

Moving to a more serious note, ask the young people how they should respond if they were trying to reach these children with the gospel. What kind of facial expressions would help them make friends with these children? What kind of gestures? What kind of inclinations in their voice? When you finish this discussion, move on to the missions segment for the meeting.

# The World Missions News Update

"The Lord announced the word, and great was the company of those who proclaimed it" (Psalm 68:11).

This is a missions news segment; a news update to keep students current with the latest news from the field.

### When to Use

- Use as a periodic update on missions (weekly, biweekly, or monthly).
- Use to begin a youth meeting.
- Use to introduce a missions message.
- Use as a missions news segment in an adult service.

## Objectives

To familiarize young people with missions publications and sources where they can find current news of missions activities, needs, accomplishments, and miracles.

To give students opportunity to research and report on missions around the world in order to increase their knowledge of, and their participation in, missions.

## Materials

☐ 1. The official magazine of a mission organization, preferably one that your church supports. It will likely report on missions activities, and give informative reports on unreached peoples. If your church does not already receive one, write to the home office of the organization or call requesting this magazine.

☐ 2. Missionary newsletters. Ask your pastor for the newsletters he receives from missionaries, or write missionaries directly requesting their newsletters. Names and addresses of missionaries can be obtained from their mission board or organization.

☐ 3. Check the news section of your denominational magazine for missions-related news.

☐ 4. Check the international section of your local newspaper for news from various countries. Adapt the information to the missions setting. For example, if there is a riot in a particular country, how will this affect our missionaries or Christians inside the country?

☐ 5. Purchase a large world map or globe so that the students can see the places where the news is happening.

## Preparation

Subscribe to and/or gather the needed materials (as listed above).

Select a "news team." Give them a vision for the news segment. Give them materials. Tell them they have three minutes each service (or at whatever intervals you choose) to get the missions news to the other students. Train them to be quick-paced and informative. Instruct them to give only two, or at most three, news stories per segment. The students will not remember much more than three stories at a time.

Have the news team create its own name, logo, background, and theme song. Enhance the presentation with maps, charts, and pictures. If you have video equipment available, have team pre-tape part of the "news cast." Excerpts from newsletters and articles can be pre-taped and shown on the monitor as the "anchor person" reads the excerpt.

## Method

At the designated time the "news crew" must be ready to go on the "air." Have them go through their news report much like a "weekend news update" on television. Most of the work will be done in preparing for this three-minute segment. The key will be for students to practice ahead of time and to be spirited and quick with their presentation.

# PART IV

# *Taste of Missions*

This section teaches flexibility and tolerance. It also gives
the young people exposure to new foods and various ways of eating.
It introduces the concept that eating is seen as a ministry
in many parts of the world.

# Coke In A Bag

"Follow the way of love." (1 Corinthians 14:1)

Students are served soft drinks in small plastic bags; as is the practice in some cultures where the deposit on the glass bottle is very important to the store owners.

## When to Use

- Use as an attention-getter before a youth meeting.
- Use as a social event with a missions flavor after a youth meeting.
- Use at a missions retreat or convention.
- Do this for adults in the church as part of a missions emphasis.

## Objective

To demonstrate to young people that each culture has a different way of doing things by exposing them to a new cultural practice—how people from some countries drink coke.

## Materials

☐ Purchase enough assorted soft-drinks for each person. (You may want to use Kool-Aid, depending on your budget.)

☐ Purchase a plastic bag for each person. Use the "disposable bottles" found in the baby section of department stores. These are leak-proof plastic bags used as liners in disposable baby bottles.

☐ A straw for each person.

☐ Table(s) to use for a serving counter.

## Preparation

In some of the poorer countries, soft drinks still come in bottles, and the return deposits on these bottles are very valuable to the seller. In some stores and restaurants, when an order is made for coke "to go," the clerk will open the bottle, pour its contents into a plastic bag, put a straw in it and hand it to the customer. This activity is a simulation of that event.

Gather the materials needed and enlist the help of your youth workers. Set up several serving stations according to the size of your youth group.

To add cultural atmosphere, play foreign music and put up foreign decorations.

## Method

Have the students go to the serving stations to get their soft drinks. To give students the best experience, pour the soft drinks into the plastic bags as they make their individual orders so they will see it being done.

# Eat It With A Smile

"But do this with gentleness and respect." (1 Peter 3:15)

Take the students to an ethnic restaurant. Tell them to order anything they want. Prearrange with the management to feed all young people the same items regardless of what they order. Before the food arrives, explain to students how sometimes in a foreign country missionaries don't get what they order. The young people will experience what missionaries and their children sometimes experience in overseas restaurants.

## When to Use

- Use at a missions retreat.
- Use at a missions banquet.
- Use as a setting for a youth meeting.

## Objective

To give young people a simulated, cross-cultural experience which often happens to missionaries and their children. They will learn what is the appropriate response from the missionary who is a guest in that country.

## Materials

☐ An ethnic restaurant with reasonable prices.

☐ Option 1: Have youth workers or others in the congregation cook a foreign meal for the youth at the church.

☐ Option 2: Pass out ethnic finger food or snack foods that can be eaten during the meeting (choose something that leaves little or no mess).

## Preparation

Choose an ethnic restaurant; if possible, one with a private room that could seat your entire youth group. Arrange with them to serve your group a simple and unappealing meal that would be typical of their particular country. For example: British or Australian restaurants—very greasy foods such as fried eggs, sausage, and sliced beets. Korean restaurants—fried and battered squid with pickled cabbage. Chinese restaurants—lots of rice with plain cooked vegetables and just tea to drink (no soft drinks).

In many countries, drinks are served after the meal instead of during the meal.

Also arrange with the restaurant to extend all the normal services. Have the waiters take individual orders. Tell students that soft drinks cannot be ordered, since they will be unavailable in most countries.

Option 1: If you choose to have the meal prepared at church, type up a menu of three to four entrees from which the students can choose.

Option 2: If you choose to serve finger food or snack foods in the meeting, have your students form small groups and use youth workers as waiters and waitresses to go around and take orders.

## Method

Before leaving for the restaurant, explain to the young people that they will be experiencing a little bit of the missionary's world by eating in an ethnic restaurant. Outline the rules of etiquette you expect them to follow while at the restaurant.

Once everyone has arrived and is seated, tell students they may order anything they would like from the menu. After everyone has ordered, talk to them about eating in foreign countries. Ask for stories they have heard, experiences they have had, or impressions they have about food in foreign countries. Then move on to explain that sometimes when missionaries eat in a restaurant in a foreign country, they do not always get what they order, or, when their food comes, it does not look or smell like what they ordered. Ask students what they think a missionary or a member of a missionary family should do in that kind of situation. After a brief discussion, explain that in most places in our culture, it is fine to send food back to the kitchen and re-order, but as a guest in a foreign country, and especially if someone from that country is taking you out to eat, it is important that you eat whatever food is placed before you. Eat it with a smile. No complaints or rudeness can be expressed. You must avoid offending your host. End your brief discussion by inviting students to pretend that this is a foreign country, to be brave, and to eat whatever is placed in front of them.

As the food arrives, students may begin reacting with shock that, "This is not what I ordered!" Go around to the tables and remind them about not offending the host, eating everything with a smile, and seeing this as a learning experience. Laugh and have fun with this. Most of the students will follow your lead.

Follow the meal with a message and challenge about missions, depending on the time remaining.

# Eating Ministry

"Give thanks in all circumstances" (1 Thessalonians 5:16).

This activity will give students a sense of how eating food becomes a ministry unto the Lord.

## When to Use

- Use this activity to open a youth meeting.
- Use as a lead-in to the message for the evening.
- Use for a missions service with the adult congregation.
- Use at a missions retreat.

## Objective

To give young people an experience of eating unfamiliar and unappetizing food in order to help them understand how a simple thing like eating food with the right kind of attitude can be a witness for Christ.

## Materials

- ☐ Food: Choose one to three kinds of food that young people will think is terrible, such as, squid, octopus, alligator meat, pigs feet, cows' tongue, crawfish, elephant meat, etc. (Note: Your local grocery store will be able to obtain some exotic foods through its deli. Also check with local ethnic food stores that serve Oriental, Muslim, European, etc.)
- ☐ Drink: Choose a fruit juice which is unusual to your community, such as guava or mango juice.
- ☐ Small paper plates.
- ☐ Small paper cups.
- ☐ Plastic forks—this is optional. It is more realistic to eat the food with hands.
- ☐ Cooking utensils, if needed.

## Preparation

Before the meeting, take food you have chosen and cut it into bite-size pieces. Put the juice into small Dixie-size cups. Place everything on serving trays so it is ready to be served. Choose several students to pass out the food.

## Method

At the designated time in the meeting, distribute the food similarly to the way communion is distributed. Instruct students not to eat or drink until everyone has been served.

As the food and drinks are distributed, talk to students about how eating can become a ministry. You can say something like this:

"In the United States, young people consume mass quantities of food. Groups of students order large pizzas or Big Macs and stuff themselves, and it's no big deal if they leave food on their plates or throw it in the garbage when they leave the restaurant. No one is offended. No one looks down on their Christian witness. No one loses out with Christ because of it."

"However, overseas if you are invited to a home for a meal, you can offend the host by not eating all the food that has been put on your plate. In some cultures, guests are expected to take a second helping. If you don't accept their food graciously, the host family may think that you are an ungrateful American and that you serve an ungrateful God. In some Third World countries, food is more important than video games, Game Boys, skateboards, etc. In that kind of culture, eating food becomes a ministry. If you eat food graciously and with a smile, then they will think of you as a gracious person and that you serve a loving, caring God."

"We are going to practice eating food the way we would need to eat if we were in a Third World country such as Burkina Faso."

At this point, ask if everyone has been served. Explain that in some overseas cultures, it's rude to begin eating before everyone has food before them.

Next, pray and ask the Lord to bless the food and to help everyone eat what they are to eat.

Before you instruct them to eat the food, explain that it's very important for them to eat this with a "ministry face." This is a face that smiles even though the food may not taste good. With a ministry face, the guest does not screw up his or her nose and make yucky noises about the food. A ministry face smiles and tells the host "thank you."

Give the signal for everyone to eat. Without making a big issue, encourage everyone to at least try the food. Have everyone eat the meat together, followed by the juice.

After everyone is finished and you've given time to talk and laugh about their food encounter, ask for volunteers. Ask:"How did the food taste? How did it feel to eat the food? Was it slimy? Sticky? Difficult to swallow? Could you eat this food every week for four years?"

Pull together the experience at the end with a prayer asking for a greater understanding of the challenges missionaries face in leading people to Christ. You may have an opportunity to challenge the students regarding missions work, a short-term trip, or giving to missions.

# Finger-Licking Good

"The mind controlled by the Spirit is life and peace," (Romans 8:6)

In many Third World countries, people do not have dining rooms in their houses or dining tables and chairs. They will often sit on the floor and eat their food with their hands. In this activity the young people sit on the floor and eat a meal with their right hands. Soft drinks are served warm and without ice. Towels are used instead of napkins.

## When to Use

- Use at the beginning of a youth meeting.
- Use at the end of a youth meeting.
- Use at a missions retreat or convention.

## Objective

To help young people become more familiar with some of the cultural differences in other countries so they will understand how missionaries and their children feel when adjusting to a new culture.

## Materials

☐ Food: Prepare a menu that will be messy or unusual to eat with fingers, such as spaghetti, lasagna, or other foods that are usually served with a sauce.

☐ Plates and cups. No silverware is needed.

☐ Towels will replace napkins. Supply enough towels so that five people have access to one towel.

## Preparation

In your introduction, tell students about the portions of the world where cooking is done over an open fire or on wood stoves. Explain that people eat with their hands. Certain cultures, such as the Indian culture, African tribes, and Latin American tribes, eat with their hands.

To explain why students are required to eat with their right hands, tell how people from these cultures use their left hands for the "dirty jobs" in life. If students do not catch the idea, explain that this refers especially to cultures where there is no toilet paper.

Most of these cultures do not use disposable paper napkins; instead, they use cloth towels.

Choose cooks and plan out the meal. Plan to use the church's kitchen and dining hall. Set up a serving line cafeteria-style.

Designate an eating area. Move all furniture out of that area so the floor is completely clear.

## Method

Gather young people and introduce the activity by mentioning some of the background on why various people of the world eat on the floor with their hands. Give instructions about the serving line, sitting on the floor, using only the right hand, and using a towel instead of a napkin. Have them go through the food line and then eat their meal.

After the meal is finished, challenge the students with the missions topic for the evening.

# Market

"Glory, honor and peace for everyone who does good" (Romans 2:10).

In many countries, people buy food, clothing, and other items at an "open air market." With this activity, young people get first-hand experience at purchasing food items in a "market" environment. They use a "trade language" and "barter" for items. Also, just as is normal in overseas markets, prices are changed frequently.

## When to Use

- Use for an outdoor service.
- Use at the beginning of the meeting.
- Use at a missions retreat or convention.
- Optional: Use as a way to offer a meal. Instead of selling snack foods,

sell foreign meals.

## Objective

To give students opportunity to participate in a simulated experience of purchasing items at an overseas market. As a result, they will learn some of the challenges of daily living overseas.

## Materials

- ☐ Snack foods such as bite-size candy/chocolate bars, assorted candies, Kool-Aid (warm with no ice).

- ☐ A table to be used as the counter for displaying food. If you want to get elaborate, put up a booth with cloth to hang down on the sides and over the top.

- ☐ "Play money" called "megadough" (make copies of the "megadough" money provided on page 68.)

## Preparation

The previous week, instruct students to bring a dollar or two for this activity. Set up a bank for them to "exchange" their money for "megadough." All purchases at the market will have to be done in the "megadough" currency.

Purchase junk food to feed each student three to five pieces of candy and up to two cups of Kool-Aid. Make enough money for everyone to purchase a limited amount of food. Don't make them so poor that they cannot afford anything; on the other hand, don't make them so rich that they can buy out the store.

Choose one or more people to sell the food. If possible, choose someone who has had overseas experience at a market.

Plan to change prices frequently. If students are buying up certain items, raise the price so they will have to pay more for it. Lower the prices on food that is not selling.

The market uses a "barter" system in pricing. Nothing should have price tags. The final selling price is negotiated between the seller and the buyer, similar to negotiations made in purchasing a car. The seller may start with seven megadough for a cup of Kool-Aid. The buyer might start at three megadough. After bartering back and forth, the final agreed price might be set at five megadough. As a rule of thumb, settle on a final price that is about half way between the seller's and buyer's starting prices.

To make this activity feel more foreign, insist that students use an official "trade" language. In this case, a simple sign language using fingers to indicate prices will be the official trade language. Seven fingers indicate seven megadough, five fingers indicates five megadough, and so forth. Establish a rule that only those using the trade language will be served. No talking is allowed during transactions. Pretend that those selling the food do not understand English. Have them talk gibberish or a foreign language.

Plan on one "store" in the market serving 15 to 20 people. For example, if your youth group has 30 in attendance, plan on having two "stores" in your market.

To add atmosphere, decorate and play foreign music.

## Method

As students arrive, send them to the "bank" to "exchange" their money (use their American money to cover their expenses for food). At the appropriate time, explain that in this activity they will experience what missionaries and their children experience when they purchase items at the market. Explain how things are done. Then let them dive into the experience. The actual bartering should be done in silence, using only the "trade language." Help those who are having trouble. Some of the students will be shy, but set a goal of having every student buy at least one item.

When you stop the activity, have students gather together and begin a discussion focusing on their feelings while they were doing the activity. Ask what feelings they had. What was strange or different to them? How did they deal with it? How well did they like it?

# Missions Banquet

"And how can they believe in the one of whom they have not heard?" (Romans 10:14)

A formal banquet is prepared European-style. Tables are set with tablecloths and centerpieces. Place settings are arranged with two forks, two spoons, and two knives. The meal is served in five courses.

## When to Use

- Use as a setting for a regular weekly meeting.
- Use as a banquet separate from anything else.
- Use as a banquet for a special occasion such as Valentine's Day—adapt the occasion to the missions message.
- Use at a missions retreat or convention.

## Objective

To introduce young people to a very formal type of dining style, common among most upper class cultures, especially in Europe, and to promote a theme throughout the banquet which will help youth focus on missions.

## Materials

- ☐ Enough staff to cook and serve the meal.
- ☐ Church kitchen and dining hall.
- ☐ Banquet setting: tables, chairs, tablecloths, centerpieces, place settings, and decorations.
- ☐ Food: Meal suggestions

   Course One—plain salad, sprinkled lightly with salad oil, parmesan cheese, and croutons. Also provide up to three types of salad dressing.

   Course Two—soup, such as cream of mushroom.

   Course Three—meat and vegetables, such as sliced beef, French-cut beans, and corn.

   Course Four—dessert, such as ice cream.

   Course Five—cheddar cheese (mild), Ritz crackers, and tea.

- • Note: Serve water during the meal, but do not serve soft drinks, etc.

## Preparation

Decide whether you want to use this banquet as a setting for your regular weekly meeting or as a separate event.

If you choose to use this banquet as a setting for your regular weekly meeting, during the weeks prior, tell young people this will be a formal night. Encourage them to dress up. Plan your meeting around the meal. If you choose to use this banquet as a separate event, during the weeks prior, sell tickets and plan a program to follow the meal. Have your servers dress up—coat and tie for men and dresses for women. Instruct them to be polite, happy, and to smile a lot. If possible, have them speak English in some kind of foreign accent. Choose a foreign theme around which to base your decorations and music.

Table settings: Place both forks on the left of the plate with napkins folded in half underneath them. Place both knives on the right of the plate and the spoons at the top of the plate. When eating, silverware furthest from the plate is used first.

## Method

As the young people arrive, have servers escort them to their tables. Lead off with a welcome, explanation regarding the missions emphasis, and prayer. Also explain how the silverware is used.

Have the servers bring the food. Enjoy the meal. Follow the meal by the program for the rest of the banquet. End by challenging students for missions.

Option: Serve each student a bowl of rice and a glass of water for the banquet. Give them a spoon or chopsticks to eat with. For hundreds of thousands of people, this is the only meal they will have from day to day.

# Tea Time

"You must go to everyone I send you to and say whatever I command you." (Jeremiah 1:7)

This activity simulates the European tradition of having tea and cookies in the middle of the morning and the middle of the afternoon. This is practiced in many countries on all continents. In countries which have tea time, children and teenagers often participate. This works best if you focus on a particular country. For example, "Today we're going to celebrate tea time the way they do in Spain." This activity can work with a group of up to 300.

## When to Use

- Use to begin a service or a class.
- Use as a lead-in to a message on missions.
- Use to promote an upcoming short-term missions trip or other missions-oriented activities.

## Objective

To give students the experience of "break time" European style, where they will have the opportunity to try new foods and learn that the key to enjoying a cultural experience is to be adaptable.

## Materials

☐ Mix the following recipe:
Tea (coffee can be used as a substitute).
Equal amounts of tea and milk.
Add one to one and a half cups of sugar per quart.

Make it sweet to taste.
Serve lukewarm or cold.

☐ Cookies: These should be store-bought sugar cookies.

☐ Portion:
One or two swallows of tea per person. This cuts down spillage.
One cookie per person, or half a cookie per person.

## Method

Have portions prepared ahead of time for each person. Serve the tea in small paper cups. Give each person just a swallow or two. Do not tell them what they are going to be drinking. Serve cookies on a dish to be passed around. (This can follow the fashion of distributing communion elements. However, this will not be nearly as serious.) Ask: "How many enjoy a break at school or on the job?" Then go on to explain that they will be participating in a "tea time," which is the foreign equivalent to "break." Ask what they enjoy drinking and eating during their breaks. You will probably get answers like soft drinks, candy bars, chips. Explain that this time they'll be doing it differently, and they must guess what it is they're eating and drinking. While the tea and cookies are being distributed, you can explain how in a foreign home, the mother prepares things in the kitchen and puts them on a tray and the teenager carries the tray out to the guests in the living room and serves them.

Everyone should hold his or her tea and cookie and eat together. When everyone has been served, tell students to take the cookie and dunk it into the Dixie cup. After they have all tried it and talked and laughed, ask them if they would prefer to have this kind of a tea time instead of their soft drinks and junk food. Ask two or three of the students what they think they had to eat and drink. For larger groups, have selected individuals come to the front to speak into a microphone.

## Processing

Explain that in different cultures things are done differently. Food tastes different. The key to enjoying the cultural experience is to be adaptable. Ask how many of them liked their tea and cookie. Explain for those who didn't like it, that it would be an insult to the host, in a foreign culture, to say so. Many times people have to eat what they're served without making any gross gestures or comments. The most important thing is to be polite.

# PART V

# *Music, Skits and Stories*

Through these dramatic presentations, students get a
hilarious yet serious view of missions. These also
encourage participation by young people.

# Cross-Cultural Sermon

"Our gospel came to you not simply with words, but also with power."
(1 Thessalonians 1:5)

This is a humorous presentation of a Bible-thumping, foot-stomping American minister preaching in a Third World country through an interpreter. Some of the cultural differences between the United States and the cultures in which our missionaries serve are clearly illustrated.

## When to Use

- Use as an introduction to a meeting.
- Use in an adult service as a missions emphasis.
- Use during a missions convention.

## Objective

To help young people learn, through a humorous presentation of a missionary sermon, how important it is for missionaries and their families to be aware of the cultural differences that exist in a foreign environment in order to communicate the gospel effectively.

## Materials

☐ Script of the cross-cultural sermon.

## Preparation

Choose two youth to play the parts of an animated evangelist with a southern accent and an interpreter who speaks pidgin English. The interpreter can use any foreign accent, such as Indian, African, or Latin American.

Have them practice until they are familiar with the script. They could put the script in their Bible or on the pulpit, eliminating the need to memorize it.

## Method

Set up the presentation by explaining the setting and introducing the preacher and interpreter. Then sit back and enjoy.

# PREACHING THROUGH AN INTERPRETER

*A cross-cultural sermon*

*by Greg Baggs, Brent Hanson, Keith Jackson, and Shannon Smeya*

INTRODUCTION: There are many cultural differences between the United States and the countries where missionaries serve. Sometimes it can be very difficult to communicate. To help illustrate this point, we have two special guests. One is a fire-breathing evangelist; the other is his interpreter. So please pretend with me that we are overseas (name the continent you have chosen) and this evangelist is coming to minister to us. Please welcome our evangelist, Rev. _____ and his interpreter, Rev. _____.

| | |
|---|---|
| PREACHER: | Hello! |
| INTERPRETER: | Greetings! |
| PREACHER: | I feel so good to be here with you today. |
| INTERPRETER: | I'm just so healthy to be here with you today. |
| PREACHER: | I feel so good to be here with you today. |
| INTERPRETER: | I'm just so healthy to be here with you today. |
| PREACHER: | I am from Texas, the Lone Star State. |
| INTERPRETER: | Dis man is from Texas, the state with just one star in the sky. |
| PREACHER: | I'm pastor of a church of 4,000 people. |
| INTERPRETER: | Dis man pastors a church larger than our whole country. |
| PREACHER: | I must say I was nervous flying over here. |
| INTERPRETER: | Dis man was afraid to come here. |
| PREACHER: | In the Bible, Jesus says, "And lo, I am with you always." But He didn't say anything about being with us high up in an airplane. |
| INTERPRETER: | It is okay. He has just told a dumb joke. |
| PREACHER: | You people really pack a church like a can of sardines. |
| INTERPRETER: | You people have begin to look like small fish. |
| PREACHER: | I want to thank you for lunch. |
| INTERPRETER: | I would like to thank you for the lunch we have just eating. |
| PREACHER: | Eating with you is more fun than a barrel of monkeys. |
| INTERPRETER: | Eating with you is more fun than having primates in a keg. |
| PREACHER: | The Lord knows I really made a pig out of myself. |
| INTERPRETER: | God turned me into a swine. |
| PREACHER: | I must admit I had a few butterflies about eating your food. |
| INTERPRETER: | But I—what did you have? |
| PREACHER: | A few butterflies. |
| INTERPRETER: | Oh. It seems to me that our guest, he took some flies into his stomach. We are so sorry, my brother. |
| PREACHER: | Oh, no. The food was very good. The food was very good. |

INTERPRETER: You like the flies?

PREACHER: Oh, the food was very good.

INTERPRETER: He likes the flies.

PREACHER: I'm just tickled pink you shared your food with me.

INTERPRETER: Tickled pink?

PREACHER: I'm tickled pink, yes.

INTERPRETER: But it seems to me that our brother from eating this food has developed a rash and has just begun to scratch himself pink.

PREACHER: It was good to just sit around and chew the fat with you.

INTERPRETER: But it was good to just sit around and drink grease with you.

PREACHER: I'm especially ecstatic about the topic you've asked me to address today.

INTERPRETER: I am especially elastic about this topic you have asked me to undress today.

PREACHER: The topic is, "How to Get People Involved in a Spiritual Ministry."

INTERPRETER: The topic is, "How to Get People Involved in Ministering to Spirits."

PREACHER: Too many people are running around like chickens with their heads cut off.

INTERPRETER: Too many people—what they doing?

PREACHER: Running around like chickens with their heads cut off.

INTERPRETER: Oh, in dis man's country there is great persecution. They are just cutting their heads off like chickens. We will pray for you, my brother.

PREACHER: People are all caught up in the rat race of life.

INTERPRETER: People are just running 100-yard dash with rodents.

PREACHER: Their testimonies are not worth a hill of beans.

INTERPRETER: Their testimony's not worth a mountain of vegetables.

PREACHER: Part of the problem is our pastors.

INTERPRETER: Part of the problem is our pastors.

PREACHER: When they preach, they need to knock their socks off.

INTERPRETER: When they preach, they need to undress their feet.

PREACHER: But they are always jumping the gun.

INTERPRETER: But they—what are they doing now?

PREACHER: Jumping the gun.

INTERPRETER: Oh, these pastors are putting a gun down to the ground and jumping over it.

PREACHER: They're always shooting their mouths off.

INTERPRETER: No!!

PREACHER: Shooting their mouths off.

INTERPRETER: These pastors are just taking a gun, putting it to their mouths, and shooting their lips off.

| | |
|---|---|
| PREACHER: | Many times prayer is left behind. |
| INTERPRETER: | Many times prayer follows. |
| PREACHER: | Many times they have a problem being too lackadaisical. |
| INTERPRETER: | Many times they have a problem with laxatives. |
| PREACHER: | There is great disorganization in the services. |
| INTERPRETER: | Things are just run so smoothly. |
| PREACHER: | Many times people arrive an hour late. |
| INTERPRETER: | Many times people come just on time. |
| PREACHER: | I know how it is to get ready for Sunday services. |
| INTERPRETER: | I also know how it is to get ready for church on a Sunday. |
| PREACHER: | You try to get ready, and the kids are in the backyard, as filthy as pigs. |
| INTERPRETER: | What has happened? |
| PREACHER: | You try to get ready, but many times the kids are in the backyard, as filthy as pigs. |
| INTERPRETER: | Oh. You try to get ready, and there are some baby goats in the backyard and they begin to look like pigs. |
| PREACHER: | You bring them into the house and put them in the tub. |
| INTERPRETER: | You do? Then you bring these baby goats into your house and put them in the tub. |
| PREACHER: | These kids begin to climb the wall. |
| INTERPRETER: | But the baby goats escape. |
| PREACHER: | Finally you're ready for church. |
| INTERPRETER: | Thank God. Finally you are ready for church. |
| PREACHER: | You step outside, and it's raining cats and dogs. |
| INTERPRETER: | You step—what's it doing now? |
| PREACHER: | It's raining cats and dogs. |
| INTERPRETER: | You step outside, and small animals begin to fall from the sky. |
| PREACHER: | It's enough to make your head spin. |
| INTERPRETER: | It's enough to make his head rotate. |
| PREACHER: | It's too much for you, and you get mad at your wife and kids. |
| INTERPRETER: | It's just too much for you, and you sin against your wife and these baby goats. |
| PREACHER: | You chew your wife out. |
| INTERPRETER: | You begin to bite your wife. |
| PREACHER: | Finally you get to church, but you're not thinking about God. |
| INTERPRETER: | Finally you come into the house of God, but you are not thinking about Him. |
| PREACHER: | You look over the congregation, and people are just sitting there like knots on a log. |
| INTERPRETER: | You look over this congregation. People are just sitting there like holes in wood. |

| | |
|---|---|
| PREACHER: | You look over at your wife, and she's trying to smile. |
| INTERPRETER: | You look over at your wife, and she's just trying to grin. |
| PREACHER: | But everyone can tell that you've just chewed her out. |
| INTERPRETER: | But everyone can see the blood is just dripping down where you have just bitten her. |
| PREACHER: | That's not serving God. Give me a break! |
| INTERPRETER: | That's not serving God. Hit me in the face! |
| PREACHER: | That's just a bunch of bologna. |
| INTERPRETER: | That's just a sandwich. |
| PREACHER: | Sometimes our attitude about serving God is not a bowl of cherries. Sometimes it's just the pits. |
| INTERPRETER: | Sometimes our attitude about serving God is not a bowl of fruit. Sometimes it's under your arms. |
| PREACHER: | Sometimes you just need to blow off steam. |
| INTERPRETER: | Sometimes you need to put your lips on a bowl of boiling water and just blow. |
| PREACHER: | You need to get on fire for Jesus. |
| INTERPRETER: | You need to just burn yourself for Jesus. |
| PREACHER: | But it seems like someone is always there to quench the fire. |
| INTERPRETER: | But, thank God, somebody comes and puts you out before you burn to death. |
| PREACHER: | What we need is people with enough guts to fast and pray. |
| INTERPRETER: | What we need is you people with the big bellies to fast and pray. |
| PREACHER: | You need to fast and pray the house down. |
| INTERPRETER: | You need to fast and pray until this house of Satan falls down. |
| PREACHER: | We don't need flaming evangelists in our church. |
| INTERPRETER: | We don't need you to burn your evangelist when he comes to your church. |
| PREACHER: | You need to get into the closet of prayer. |
| INTERPRETER: | Where? |
| PREACHER: | Into the closet. |
| INTERPRETER: | Water closet? |
| PREACHER: | Yes, closet. |
| INTERPRETER: | Go to your toilets and pray. |
| PREACHER: | Get under the spout where the glory comes out. |
| INTERPRETER: | Even if you have to get in the shower and pray, do it. |
| PREACHER: | Baby, say Jesus! |
| INTERPRETER: | Infants praise the Lord. |
| PREACHER: | Now I can see that time is flying, and I must rush to a conclusion. |
| INTERPRETER: | You saw it? Dis man had a vision. He saw time was just flying like this, and while he was looking at it, he drove into a conclusion. |

| | |
|---|---|
| PREACHER: | If you will follow my words . . . |
| INTERPRETER: | If you will talk like I do . . . |
| PREACHER: | The power of God will sweep over you. |
| INTERPRETER: | God will hit you with a broom. |
| PREACHER: | The power of God will sweep over your congregation. |
| INTERPRETER: | God will hit your congregation with a broom. |
| PREACHER: | And you will find yourself spiritually walking in the Promised Land. Glory! |
| INTERPRETER: | And you will find yourself dead and gone to heaven. |
| PREACHER: | Now every word I've spoken tonight is true, and you can find it in the Bible. |
| INTERPRETER: | Dis man just believes everything he has taught us tonight is in the Bible. |
| PREACHER: | I hope someday some of you can come to America and help us as much as I've helped you tonight. |
| INTERPRETER: | My brothers, I hope that someday you can come to America and just straighten this man's theology out. |
| PREACHER: | God bless you, and keep on truckin'! |
| INTERPRETER: | God bless the truck drivers. |
| PREACHER: | Amen! |
| INTERPRETER: | Thank God! He is finished. Amen! |

# Grip of Sin

"The Spirit of the Lord is on me . . . to proclaim freedom for the prisoners." (Luke 4:18)

Students act out a mime about the grip sin can have over an individual's life. A missionary's prayer breaks the bondage of sin.

## When to Use

- Use as a missions segment for a youth meeting.
- Use in an adult service as a missions emphasis.
- Use during a missions convention.

## Objectives

To show students how the attractiveness of sin is a trap that renders people powerless to free themselves. This will help them recognize again the sinner's need of a Savior.

To demonstrate to young people that human might and intelligence cannot release the grip of sin. As a result they will understand the importance of the missionary's role in introducing people to the One who can free the world from the bondage of sin.

## Materials

- ☐ Piano, keyboard, or musical soundtrack to be played during the mime.
- ☐ Costumes for the characters.
- ☐ No background set is needed.

## Preparation

The skit requires several individuals to act out the following roles:

A human apple tree with an apple in each hand.

Several characters who dress as foreigners from a variety of countries.

A missionary.

## Method

A gorgeous-looking apple tree walks to center stage and holds out the delicious-looking apples. The tree symbolizes the tree in the garden of Eden from which Adam and Eve ate. Individually and in pairs, the foreign characters enter the stage. The first individual is enamored by the tree's beauty. He steps up for a closer look. To his delight, he notices the apples and reaches out for one, but withdraws his hand as he struggles with the temptation to take it. Finally, he gives in to the temptation and takes hold of the apple. To his surprise the apple will not come loose. Not yet realizing that he is stuck to the apple, with his other hand, he reaches for the branch (the tree's arm) to apply more strength. This time he is surprised that he is truly stuck to the tree. He struggles, but cannot free himself.

While he struggles, the next character walks out. He sees the situation and goes to help. As he touches the first character, he gets stuck. In his struggle to free himself, he grabs hold of the tree and gets stuck to it as well. Neither person can free himself.

As they continue to struggle, additional characters come on to the stage to help, but find themselves stuck to the tree and to those already stuck.

Finally, a missionary enters. He surmises the situation and decides prayer is needed rather than human might and intelligence. As he prays, one by one the characters come loose from the tree. They are delighted and thank the missionary as they all exit the stage.

As a variation, characters could represent various religions such as Islam,

Buddhism, Hinduism, and others. After all these fail to free the people from the tree, the missionary enters, prays, and they are freed.

# Human Slide Show

"'Come, follow me,' Jesus said, 'and I will make you fishers of men.'" (Mark 1:17)

Missionaries have been notorious for their slide presentations. This slide presentation is done with real people who "freeze" for each slide. It is narrated by a student acting as a missionary.

## When to Use

- Use at the beginning of a meeting.
- Use before a missions message.
- Use in an adult service.
- Use at a missions retreat or convention.

## Objectives

To focus the attention of young people on missions, through the use of a humorous presentation of a missionary slide show, in order that they can learn about various aspects of missionary life.

## Materials

☐ One white sheet or large tablecloth.

## Preparation

The idea is to use a typical missionary slide presentation format to depict various aspects of missions, such as comical aspects of missionary life overseas, itinerating in the States, school overseas, cross-cultural shock, or aspects of your youth group's participation in various missions activities. Instead of slides, use real people.

Plan on five to seven "slides." Choose someone to be the missionary and narrate the slides. Write a script. Have your students practice.

For the slide show, have two people hold up the sheet. The actors for each slide get in position behind the sheet. This is going on while the "missionary" gives a narration. When he gives the signal, the two people holding the sheet drop it to the floor, allowing the audience to see what the missionary is talking about. When he signals again, the two people bring the sheet back up and the actors change to a new position for the next slide.

## Method

At the appropriate time during the meeting, introduce the "missionary" as a special guest. Introduce him as a pastor would introduce a real missionary. Give the "missionary" a typical pastoral hug. Then let the "missionary" do his thing.

# Missions Stories

"Respect those who work hard among you . . . hold them in the highest regard in love because of their work." (1 Thessalonians 5:12-13)

Students listen to stories about missions—the people, culture, miracles, and missionaries.

## When to Use

- Use before a message.
- Use as a follow-up to a message.

## Objective

To inform young people about some heroes and miracles of missions so that they may be challenged to become involved in missions.

## Materials

☐ None.

## Preparation

Order books regarding missions. Look through books that tell stories about miracles, how people receive Christ, missionary highlights, and biographies. Check with the William Carey Library in Pasadena, California.

Also, check with your denomination's foreign missions department or office. Among the books you choose, consider obtaining C. Peter Wagner's book, *The Third Wave* and *The Pineapple Story*, published by the Bill Gothard Organization.

Read the stories to familiarize yourself with them. Write out follow-up questions for discussion and to challenge students.

Decide who will read the story—yourself, a youth worker, or a student.

Choose someone who can read well and can put a lot of expression into the story.

### Method

Have the story read at the appropriate time. Follow up with discussion, or challenge the youth about what they have just heard.

# People Need the Lord

"Go out to the roads and the country lanes, and make them come in." (Luke 14:23)

Students act out a serious mime presentation set to the song "People Need the Lord."

### When to Use

- Use at the end of a praise and worship portion of a service.
- Use to lead into a missions message.
- Use to lead into prayer time.
- Use as a presentation in an adult service or missions convention.

### Objective

To impact young people, through the use of dramatic mime, with the realization that many different kinds of people need the Lord in a worldwide context, so that youth will consider their role in taking the gospel to the world.

### Materials

☐ Music and song sheets for "People Need the Lord." These can be purchased at a local Christian book and music store.

☐ Costumes for the various characters to be portrayed in the mime.

### Preparation

The idea is to have several young people portray different kinds of people, from various countries, who need the Lord. For example: a disabled person, deaf person, a blind person, a drug addict, an alcoholic, a street person, children, prostitutes, people of different religions (such as Muslim, Hindu, Buddhist, or a tribal animist). One by one, these people walk from the back of the congregation to the front while the song is playing. Time it so that people are coming forward throughout the duration of the song. At the front, a student portrays Jesus, who reaches out to the people and helps them up onto the platform. There He heals them, they accept Him as Savior, and He embraces them. The people change expression from sad and depressed to happy.

Each person "freezes" as the next person approaches. Then the same scenario is repeated. The people stay frozen until the end of the song. At that time, all of them turn to Jesus in unison, and lift their hands towards Him as the last notes of the song fade.

Choose young people for the various parts. Have one or more students sing the song; or simply play the recording. Practice several times to get the timing, expressions, and placement smoothed out.

## Method

Introduce the presentation by talking about people around the world who need the Lord. Here are some statistics about people's needs.

67 percent of the world's population is non-Christian.

24 percent of the world's population is unevangelized.

600 million people are on the verge of starvation.

200 million people are homeless street children.

More than 20 million people have AIDS.

1.2 billion people are Muslims.

859 million people are Hindus.

359 million people are Buddhists.

101 people are tribal religionists.[4]

# Songs and Raps

"Let the Word of Christ dwell in you richly as you . . . sing psalms, hymns and spiritual songs. . . ." (Colossians 3:16)

In small groups, young people write missions-related lyrics to go along with familiar tunes, jingles or raps.

## When to Use

- Use as a missions segment for a youth meeting.
- Use at a missions retreat.

## Objective

To focus students' attention on the missions theme by encouraging them to illustrate the theme creatively through music or rap.

## Materials

☐ A sheet of paper and a pencil for each small group.

## Preparation

In this activity, young people write their own lyrics about missions, which are set to familiar tunes such as "Home on the Range," "It's a Small, Small World," "Twelve Days of Christmas," "Theme to 'Gilligan's Island,'" etc. Use tunes that would be familiar to students.

Choose a missions-related topic for the evening around which students will center their lyrics. Explain the activity to your youth workers. You may need to have them work with small groups.

## Method

Have students form small groups and then explain the activity. Read or sing one of the sample songs or raps provided. Give students a time limit and have them get started. Have the youth workers help the groups as needed.

At the end of the allotted time, have each group sing their song, or do their rap, for everyone. Optional: Instead of having small groups create their own lyrics, choose some students to sing the songs or do the raps from those provided below.

# EXAMPLES OF SONGS AND RAPS

*Use these as they are, change the words to fit your situation, or create your own.*

**Home, Home on the Field**
(Sung to the tune of "Home on the Range.")

Oh, give me a home, where the missionaries roam,
Where the MKs and natives all play,
Where the gospel is heard, and we swallow God's Word,
And give praise at the end of the day.

---

Home, home on the field,
Where the cars and the taxis don't yield.
Where seldom is heard a correct English word,
    (Pause: One person steps forward and says with a foreign accent:
    "Execute me please, mister, what time is my name?")
And the food does not look a meal.


## I'm Dreaming of a Fun Furlough
(Sung to the tune of "I'm Dreaming of a White Christmas.")

I'm dreaming of a fun furlough
Just like the ones I never knew
Filled with very short sermons,
Knowing all the new choruses,
And making friends I never knew.

I'm dreaming of a fun furlough
Leaving all the boring ones behind.
So if bright and cheery faces will smile
And think of great new dreams with every mile.


## It's a Wild World
(Sung to the tune of "It's a Small, Small World.")

It's a world of beans and rice,
A world of island life,
A world of hot, hot spice,
A world of bugs and lice,
A world of sushi,
And safari through the 'bushi,'

It's a wild world after all.
It's a wild world after all.
It's a wild world after all.
It's a wild world after all.
It's a wild, wild world.


## 12 Days Overseas
(Sung to the tune of "The 12 Days of Christmas.")

On the first day in _____ the people gave to us:
                        *(Name of country or continent)*
Day 12:  sushi burgers (or elephant burgers, etc.—hold up yucky-looking burgers)
Day 11:  guitars clanging (a student clanging an out-of-tune guitar)
Day 10:  drums a-beating (several students beat on drums, chair, table, etc.)
Day 9:   insects biting (students slap themselves and swat at imaginary flying insects)
Day 8:   ring worms spreading (draw red rings on several students' arms)
Day 7:   clouds of smog (everyone coughs)
Day 6:   crowded buses (scrunch together)
Day 5:   irritating horns (students imitate a variety of car horns)
Day 4:   dogs a howling (four kids howl)
Day 3:   roasting pigs (three students oink like pigs)
Day 2:   fighting cocks (two students crow like cocks)
Day 1:   and a big bowl of fish and rice (large bowl of rice with a foot-long fish
         laying over the top)

Make up sounds, actions or posters to illustrate the lyrics.


**Bwana, Bwana, If You Please**
(Done to a military rap-style, with echo.)

| | |
|---|---|
| Leader: | Bwana, Bwana, if you please. |
| Youth: | (echo) |
| Leader: | Give us tickets for overseas. |
| Youth: | (echo) |
| Leader: | We ready to fight with all our might. |
| Youth: | (echo) |
| Leader: | To show the world His glorious light. |
| Youth: | (echo) |
| | |
| Leader: | Sound off! |
| Youth: | One. Two. |
| Leader: | Sound off! |
| Youth: | Three. Four. |
| Leader: | Bring it on down! |
| Youth: | One, two, three, four. |
| | One-two! Three-four! |
| | |
| Leader: | Army soldiers think they're tough. |
| Youth: | (echo) |
| Leader: | But with the Spirit we've got the stuff. |
| Youth: | (echo) |
| Leader: | We can't be stopped; we're on a roll. |
| Youth: | (echo) |
| Leader: | Missions life will make us grow! |
| Youth: | (echo) |
| | |
| Leader: | Sound off! |
| Youth: | One. Two. |
| Leader: | Sound off! |
| Youth: | Three. Four. |
| Leader: | Bring it on down! |
| Youth: | One, two, three, four. |
| | One-two! Three-four! |

# PART VI

## *Services*

This section outlines actual foreign worship services.
Cross-cultural elements are included.

# African-Style Church

"On arriving there, they gathered the church together and reported all that God had done through them. . . ." (Acts 14:27)

Elements of an African service, such as the seating arrangement and music, are incorporated into the youth meeting to give it a foreign flavor.

## When to Use

- Use to begin a youth meeting.
- Use in a missions retreat or convention.

## Objective

To involve students in a simulated African church service so they can experience what ministry to Africans and people of other cultures is like for a missionary.

## Materials

- ☐ Hand drums to play during the singing.
- ☐ Optional: Wooden boards for seating.

## Preparation

Set up the room to give an African "feel." Many African congregations sit on wooden planks with no backrests. If you choose to set up wooden planks for seating, arrange them so there is an aisle down the middle. Otherwise, have the youth sit on the floor or on their regular chairs.

Arrange the seating so the guys sit on one side of the center aisle and the girls sit on the other side. Inform your staff and give them directions on how to seat the students.

Choose upbeat songs and have several students to play the hand drums during the "African" portion of the song service.

Optional: If you choose to collect the offering African-style, have a large "offering basket" at the front and have students to walk down the aisle and give their money. (See activity "Bring-it-on-Down.")

To add atmosphere, play African music before the meeting begins.

### Method

As students arrive, have the workers direct girls to sit on one side and guys to sit on the other. Explain that the meeting will have an African flavor. Then proceed with the songs, accompanied only by the drummers. If you have chosen to collect the offering African-style, give them instructions, and sing a lively song as they give.

# Bring-it-on-down Offering

"Whoever sows sparingly will also reap sparingly, and whoever sows generously will also reap generously." (2 Corinthians 9:6)

In many underdeveloped countries, especially in Africa, people bring their offerings to the front and leave them. The offering is taken this way because the things people bring would not fit into an offering plate. Focus on a country like Zaire and tell students, "Today we are going to give our offering as the Christians do in some churches in Zaire."

### When to Use

- Use this activity as a way to collect food for a food drive.
- Use it before a message dealing with commitment, materialism, or cheerful giving. Use the Scripture about the widow who gives two mites in the offering. Or, use 2 Corinthians 9:6-9 about giving because you want to—cheerfully.
- Use it after a message.
- Use it before praise and worship to emphasize thankfulness.
- Use it to promote a missions organization.

### Objectives

To provide young people the experience of giving their offering in the same manner as it is sometimes done in overseas churches so they can recognize the true sacrifice that giving represents for many Christians in other countries.

To show students the kinds of offerings overseas Christians often bring to God. As a result, young people will recognize the material blessings they have.

## Materials

☐ Clear an area in front of the pulpit/podium for students to leave their offerings.

☐ A sheet or blanket can be laid out on the floor or on a large table.

☐ Option: Announce, the previous week, that for the offering at the next youth service, students should bring food items, such as canned goods or perishables (corn on the cob, eggs, carrots, potatoes, apples, oranges, pineapple, etc.)

## Method

Explain that in some overseas churches, people walk to the front to give their offerings. In village churches, not everyone has money, so they bring whatever they grow, raise, or trade at the market. In collecting the offering, not everyone comes up at one time. They come by rows, sometimes starting at the back, sometimes starting at the front. They come forward down the middle aisle and return to their seats, using the outside aisle.

While the offering is being taken, the entire congregation stands and sings a chorus until everyone has given. Choose a lively chorus such as "What a Mighty God We Serve." Sing it acappella, over and over, until the offering is completed.

At the end of the offering, emphasize how blessed we are, and ask if any would be willing to put their computers, radios, VCRs, cars, etc., in the offering. Another challenge would be to ask if any would be willing to offer themselves to God for whatever He would want. In Africa, a teenage boy had nothing to give. He walked to the front and, stepping onto the blanket, offered himself to God.

# Communion: "I Have Not Been Served"

"How beautiful are the feet of those who bring good news!" (Romans 10:15)

This way of having communion will give young people a new realization of the masses of people around the world who still have not heard an adequate message of Jesus Christ.

## When to Use

- Use as a lead-in to a message.
- Use as a lead-in to an altar service, a dedication, call to missions, commitment, salvation, etc.
- Use as a variation of a normal communion service.

## Objective

To give students a unique presentation, during the serving of communion, that will cause them to recognize how many unreached people groups have not received the gospel. As a result, they will be confronted with their responsibility regarding the Great Commission.

## Materials

☐ You'll need communion emblems for everyone present. Use individual serving cups.

## Preparation

Before the service, choose several willing young people who would stand and make a declaration during communion. When you ask, "Has everyone been served?" they are to stand [in sequence—one at a time] and shout, "No, I have not been served! I represent the one billion Muslims who have not had an adequate witness of the gospel." They are to sit back down; then the next person stand and shout his or her declaration. Type the statements like the one above on 3″ x 5″ cards and have them ready to give to volunteers. Use the following list of unreached peoples. Other suggestions: children, homeless/orphans, the starving in famine areas, etc. Use the following list.

| Unreached Peoples | 1990 | 2000 |
|---|---|---|
| Muslims | 935 million | 1.2 billion |
| Hindus | 705 million | 859 million |
| Buddhist | 705 million | 859 million |
| Chinese Folk Religionist | 180 million | 258 million |
| Asian New Religionist | 118 million | 138 million |
| Tribal Religionist | 99 million | 101 million |
| Jews | 18 million | 24 million |
| Non Christian Spiritists | 8 million | 13 million |
| Bahais | 5 million | 8 million |
| | | |
| **Children and Youth** | | |
| Infants and children under 5 | 630 million | 693.9 million |
| Children and youth under 15 | 1.75 billion | 1.957 billion |
| Youth (age 15-24) | 1.011 billion | 1.009 billion |

*(Note: 50% of world evangelized; Reduce Children and Youth figures by 50% to arrive at unreached Children and Youth.)*

---

| Human Need | 1990 | 2000 |
|---|---|---|
| Homeless street children | 100 million | 200 million |
| AIDS carriers | 60 million | 50-200 million |
| On the verge of starvation | 400 million | 600 million |
| Urban poor | 1.27 million | 2.0 billion |
| Slum dweller | 520 million | 1.3 billion |
| Without medical care | 1.5 billion | 1.8 billion |
| Unsafe water | 1.3 billion | 3.2 billion |
| Psychotics | 51 million | 62 million |
| Drug addicts | 55 million | ? |
| Alcoholics | 170 million | ? |

Source: David B. Barrett and Todd M. Johnson, *Our Globe and How to Reach It: Seeing the World Evangelized by A.D. 2000 and Beyond* (Birmingham, Ala.: New Hope,1990). Pages 14, 24, and 36.

## Method

Serve communion in the usual way, using individual cups. When everyone has been served but is still holding the emblems ask, "Has everyone been served?" At that time, the prearranged young people should stand, one at a time, and shout their declarations.

When the last volunteer has been seated, make a brief statement about the lostness of the world. Many times young people take communion for granted, without thinking much about its meaning. However, there are millions who do not know what it is to experience the daily communion and fellowship of Jesus Christ.

Ask them if God is calling any of them to the mission field. Romans 10:14-15 can be used. How can people believe unless someone is sent to bring them the gospel?

When you have finished a brief message, finish communion.

# Underground Service

"But the Lord stood at my side and gave me strength, so that through me the message might be fully proclaimed." (2 Timothy 4:17)

In some countries, Christians must hold underground meetings. This is especially true in areas with a strong Muslim presence, or where people are hostile toward Christianity. Elements of such a service are incorporated into the youth meeting.

## When to Use

- Use as the overall setting for a youth meeting.
- Use at a missions retreat or convention.

## Objective

To portray for young people the atmosphere of an underground meeting held by Christians in some countries. Students will gain a better understanding of the risks some Christians face.

## Materials

☐ None.

## Preparation

This meeting needs to feel closed in, quiet, secretive, and at risk. Therefore, keep things simple, rather than elaborate; quiet, rather than loud. Do not use a P.A. system. Do not use instruments to accompany singing. Darken windows, if needed. Close windows. Close curtains. Dim the lights, or use fewer lights. Use subdued songs written in minor keys and songs written in rounds.

## Method

Explain to young people what kind of meeting you have planned. Instruct students to move quietly when they move, and to speak softly. Use a quiet, subdued tone when you speak. Sing quietly, without clapping. Challenge students concerning the millions of people who live under persecution.

Optional: Plan for soldiers or terrorists to interrupt the service, terrorize the congregation, and take the youth pastor to be thrown in jail or executed.

# PART VII

## *Prayer*

These prayer activities encourage young people to pray actively
for the world and also help them gather information so they
will be informed when they pray.

# Huddle Prayers

"I pray also for those who will believe in me through their message" (John 17:20).

Young people pray for world needs in small groups by forming a huddle, similar to a football huddle.

## When to Use

- Use as a prayer time for a youth meeting.
- Use at a missions retreat.

## Objectives

To encourage the participation of young people in prayer by involving them in a prayer group format which promotes closeness and the sharing of prayer needs.

To inform young people, through the use of prayer groups, of missions needs around the world so they can pray more effectively.

## Materials

☐ None.

## Preparation

In this activity, young people form "football-type" prayer huddles. This brings a closeness in sharing prayer needs. It is best if a prayer leader is assigned before the service for each huddle. Select students or youth workers to lead each small group in a prayer huddle.

Prepare a list of prayer needs. Check with your church missions board, missionaries visiting your church, the denomination's missions magazine/periodical, or a missions prayer book such as *Operation World*.[5]

## Method

Begin with a devotion or illustration of answered prayer. Emphasize the importance of prayer. Have young people form small groups with their prayer leaders. Assign prayer needs to each group as they form their prayer huddles and pray.

This can be followed by a time of prayer for the specific personal needs, school needs, etc. of the students present.

# List Prayers

"Pray also for me, that whenever I open my mouth, words may be given me so that I will fearlessly make known the mystery of the gospel" (Ephesians 6:19).

In small groups, young people list prayer needs that come to mind. Each group shares their prayer requests with the whole group. This is followed by a time of prayer.

## When to Use

- Use as the prayer time or altar service for a youth meeting.
- Use at a missions retreat.

## Objective

To help students focus on particular missions needs by asking them to list as many prayer needs as they can think of on an assigned topic within a set time frame.

## Materials

- ☐ 4" x 6" index cards and pencils for each small group.

## Preparation

The idea behind this activity is to involve students in prayer by having them list as many prayer needs as possible on a missions topic in a two minute period. This is followed by a share-and-prayer time.

Gather materials and explain the activity to youth workers. They may need to move from group to group to assist.

Prepare an introduction regarding prayer. Decide on a prayer topic; either something general like "missions" or something more specific such as a certain country or people group.

## Method

Begin this activity with a short challenge regarding prayer. Convey to students the importance of prayer. Encourage them to take this seriously.

Have students form small groups. Distribute one index card and pencil to each group. Then have the groups choose a person to write down the prayer needs. Give them two minutes (or more time if needed) to list as many prayer needs as come to mind.

Each group should then choose a spokesperson to read the list to the whole group. Close with prayer in the small groups followed by one person leading all the students in prayer.

# Poster Board Prayers

"We do not know what we ought to pray, but the Spirit himself intercedes for us." (Romans 8:26)

In this prayer activity, students form small groups, write a collective prayer on a sheet of poster board, then read the prayer to the entire youth group.

## When to Use

- Use as a prayer time for a missions retreat or convention.

## Objective

To introduce young people to a new type of prayer time. As a result they will learn how to better interact with each other as well as with God.

## Materials

☐ A sheet of poster board and marking pen for each small group.

## Preparation

Choose prayer topics for each small group, such as prayer for people groups, missionaries, children of missionaries, missions projects, countries, and world problems. The idea of this activity is to form small groups and have each member of the group write a one-sentence prayer on the poster board.

When all the prayers are completed, each group reads its prayer aloud collectively so everyone in the larger group can hear them and pray with them.

Gather the materials, explain this prayer activity to your youth leaders. Prepare them to mingle with the groups to help them during the activity.

Decide what you want to do with the poster boards after the prayer time. Here are some suggestions: Collect them and stack them at the front of the meeting area, have students surround them and lead in prayer for all the needs represented in the stack; put them up around the room for the next month to emphasize missions and as a way of checking on their prayers; keep them for one year and then bring them out and check which ones have been answered.

## Method

Explain to young people that, for prayer time, they will be praying in a new and radical way. No one will close eyes and, during parts of the prayer time, they will be writing and talking amongst themselves.

Divide them into small groups and give them instructions about the prayer activity. Have the youth leaders spread out and work with the groups.

# Prayer Cards

"Pray continually" (1 Thessalonians 5:17).

Young people create their own prayer cards to use as reminders to pray for specific missionary needs during the week.

## When to Use

- Use as prayer time for a youth meeting.
- Use to conclude and challenge young people about the importance of prayer for missions.

## Objective

To help young people prepare index cards containing specific missionary prayer needs for each day of the week. They will take them home to use as a reminder to pray daily for these needs.

## Materials

☐ 4″ x 6″ index cards and pencils for each person.
☐ Optional: Colored markers (thin point).

## Preparation

This activity can be done individually or in small groups. If you choose to do it in small groups, have everyone in the group write down the same prayer needs.

Decide what prayer needs you want students to pray about, for example: different countries of the world, people groups, missionaries, children of missionaries, specific needs known by your missions board, specific needs known to students. Write these on an overhead transparency, a chalk board, or type them on a sheet of paper and make copies to hand out to students. Either assign the prayer needs to the individuals or groups, or let students choose.

Gather materials and explain to your youth workers how you want to do the activity.

## Method

Explain that, for the prayer time, students will write prayer needs on 4 x 6 index cards and take the cards with them as prayer reminders throughout the week. Form small groups if you have chosen to do the activity this way. Distribute index cards and pencils. Distribute the prayer needs and have students write them down. Also have students write down other prayer needs that they may be aware of and want to pray for.

Have prayer for these needs, then tell students to put the cards in a place where they will see them frequently, such as: in their purses, wallets, taped to the mirrors in their bathrooms, taped to the dashboard on their car, placed in books as bookmarks, or in their lockers at school. During the week, they can research the prayer needs and list any information regarding the country or people group connected to their prayer card. Also encourage them to add sketches or drawings to help give visual impact.

Follow up the next week with any answered prayers. You may want to extend this prayer activity for more than a week.

# Proxy Prayers

"This is the assurance we have in approaching God: that if we ask anything according to his will, he hears us." (1 John 5:1-4)

Young people individually stand in proxy for prayer needs. Other students gather around, place hands on them, and pray for the need.

## When to Use

- Use as a prayer time for a youth meeting.

- Use to conclude and challenge young people about the importance of prayer and missions.

## Objective

To give young people opportunity to stand in proxy for a missionary or group needing prayer. As a result, young people will learn to pray more specifically and to empathize with the person needing prayer.

## Materials

☐ None.

## Preparation

Choose several young people to be the "stand-ins" in this proxy prayer activity.

Gather information regarding missions prayer needs from missionary letters received by the local church missions board, a missions prayer book such as *Operation World*,[6] visiting missionaries, or other sources. Either supply this information to the selected students or have them obtain it. They will need to have it ready to share with the youth group on the night of the meeting.

## Method

Have the people who will stand in proxy for prayer share the prayer needs they represent. Then have students gather around them for prayer. Encourage students to place their hands on the prayer representatives.

There are two ways you can gather young people for prayer:

1. Have those who will stand in proxy line up across the front of the meeting area and ask students to come forward to pray for them.

2. Have students form small groups with the person who will stand in proxy in the middle of each small group.

# PART VIII

## *Missionary Contact*

This section gives suggested forums and opportunities for students to have direct contact with missionaries.

# Guest Speaker

"You did not choose me, but I chose you to go and bear fruit—fruit that will last." (John 15:16)

Invite a missionary or someone with overseas experience to share their experiences with students.

## When to Use

- Use as a missions emphasis for a youth meeting.
- Use on a missions retreat.

## Objective

To give young people opportunity to interact with people who have had firsthand missions experience. This interaction will encourage them to participate in a missions effort.

## Materials

☐ Ask the missionary what he will need su as, overhead projector, slide projector, chalk board, table for displays, etc.

## Preparation

Choose a speaker(s), such as a missionary, missionary spouse, missionary kid, a member of the youth group, a member of the adult congregation who has recently returned from an overseas missions trip, an international/foreign student, or other person with overseas experience to speak to the group.

Talk with the guest speaker several weeks in advance. Set a date and give him/her guidance about your needs and limitations; i.e. time limitations, content, and challenge. Ask the speaker to relate personal experiences rather than giving a theological basis for missions. That is, relate personal experiences that would be interesting and unique to your youth group. Encourage him/her to speak about their feelings and impressions while overseas.

Also, ask your speaker to bring interesting artifacts, slides, pictures, videos, and other things the kids could handle and ask questions about. Prepare a challenge or closing for students in case you need it.

## METHOD

At the appropriate time, introduce your speaker, giving his or her back-

---

ground. After the speaker is finished, you may want to have a question-and-answer time or challenge students regarding what they learned from the speaker.

# Interview

"If you love me, you will obey what I command." (John 14:15)

An interview is conducted during a youth meeting with a missionary or some other person who has had missions experience.

## When to Use

- Use as a missions segment in a youth meeting.
- Use during Sunday School or educational time with young people.

## Objective

To expose students to a person with actual ministry experience overseas so that they will have opportunity to ask questions of the person and to learn more about missions.

## Materials

☐ None.

## Preparation

Chose a person to interview. Contact the person well in advance, get background information for the interview, and ask some questions you plan on asking during the interview. Also, ask the person to bring artifacts from the country or countries where he/she ministered. Prepare the interview questions before the actual interview.

Possible persons to interview: missionary, missionary spouse, missionary kid, or a teenager or an adult who has recently returned from a missions trip.

Optional: Have someone play the role of Paul the Apostle, and interview him regarding his missions trips in the New Testament; or have someone play the role of an historical missionary such as Hudson Taylor. (Check with the William Carey Library for biographies on historical missionaries.)

## Method

At the appropriate time during the meeting, conduct the interview. Begin with your prepared questions and add questions or change to new questions as needed. Encourage students to ask questions as well.

# Missionary Home Video

"God . . . will not forget your work and the love you have shown him as you have helped his people." (Hebrews 6:10)

Students view a home video made by a missionary or a missionary's teenage family member about their life and ministry overseas.

## When to Use

- Use as a missions segment for a youth meeting.
- Use at a missions retreat.

## Objective

To provide young people an opportunity to watch actual scenes from missionary life so they will have a "feel" of life overseas and become more aware of world needs.

## Materials

☐ TV and VCR (the mission will bring the video).

## Preparation

Months in advance, make arrangements with a missionary who has access to a VHS camcorder to videotape aspects of his or her family's life and ministry overseas. If the missionary has teenagers, request that the teen shoot, narrate, and be like a "reporter on the scene." This will give added interest for your young people.

It will help the missionary if you give him ideas for specific things to shoot. Ask for scenes in three categories: family/teen life, unique cultural differences between what American teens are used to and what is done in a foreign country, and the main thrust of the missionary's ministry.

The following is a suggested list of things to videotape:

McDonald's restaurants or other American-type restaurants in the foreign country.

Schools—include such things as buildings, uniforms, class rules, and sports.

Contrast shots of how the rich live with how the poor live.

The open market with close-ups of the meat and fish markets.

Different types of food.

Different types of unique clothing.

A church service.

Children and teens.

Various customs, such as the way people eat.

Traffic—show how wild the traffic can be.

The crowded buses and other transportation, as well as air pollution caused by cars.

Prices on a variety of items, such as a stereo, Nintendo, a glass of Coke, etc.

Ask the missionary to show you these things on the video, rather than just commenting about them.

Option: Make arrangements with a missions school for a class to do this kind of video as a class project. When you receive the video, be sure to review it. Your students may not be interested in the entire video. You may want to edit it, skip portions of it when you show it to students, or you may choose to show portions of it over a two-to four-week period.

Note: Keep your selections short; otherwise, you may lose students' attention.

## Method

At the appropriate time: show the video, stopping at points you would like to highlight. Comment on them or open it up for discussion; then move on to the next selection.

Close with a challenge regarding what students have seen.

# Phone-a-missionary

"If anyone serves, he should do it with the strength God provides, so that in all things God may be praised through Jesus Christ." (1 Peter 4:11)

With today's telephone technology, you can phone a missionary and do a telephone interview/conversation. The entire youth group can listen and participate.

## When to Use

- Use as a missions segment for a youth meeting.
- Use at a missions retreat or convention.

## Objective

To offer young people opportunity to visit with a missionary by phone. This interaction will impress upon students the reality of missionaries' work and needs.

## Materials

☐ Telephone. Patch it into your P.A. system or use a speaker phone.

## Preparation

Choose a missionary you would like to call. Check with the international operator concerning rates and international time zone changes.

Call the missionary ahead of time to make arrangements for the phone call. Discuss the questions you will ask him during the youth meeting. Talk with other family members you will want to speak with during the meeting. Set a time limit with the missionary. This will help him know how much time to spend on each question.

The key to making this phone call succeed will be asking questions that will get an interesting answer. Although calling overseas is less expensive now than it has been in the past, it is still much more expensive than calling long-distance in the United States. So, be brief with your questions, and ask the missionary to give brief answers.

To enhance the conversation, obtain a slide of the missionary family and show it during the phone conversation so the young people can see the people with whom they are talking.

To set up the telephone in the meeting room, run an extension cord from the nearest telephone jack. Plug the phone through the P.A. system so everyone can hear both sides of the conversation. You may have to purchase the necessary connections and adapters.

Option: If calling a missionary in a foreign country is too expensive for your budget, call one who is on furlough or who is itinerating in the United States.

## Method

At the appropriate time, make the call. It will be interesting for students to hear you place the call, whether you dial direct or make the call through an operator.

Go through the conversation as planned.

Close with a brief prayer for the missionary family and end with a cheer from the youth group.

# PART IX

# *Financial Giving*

This section deals with offering students a systematic way
to participate in the global missions effort through financial giving.

# Faith Promise

"Give, and it will be given to you." (Luke 6:38)

A "faith promise" is a pre-planned, systematic way of giving money to missions. Through this activity, young people pledge to give specific amounts to missions on a weekly or monthly basis.

## When to Use

- Use at the end of a missions message.
- Use at a missions convention for your young people.

## Objectives

To introduce students to a systematic method of giving money to missions which will help them give to missions regularly.

To explain to students how the faith promise works. As a result, they will be challenged to trust God to help them with their financial commitment toward missions.

## Materials

- ☐ A faith promise pledge form for each student (copy the one provided).
- ☐ A pencil for each person.

## Preparation

A faith promise is a financial pledge—an agreement a person makes with God to give a set amount to missions, usually on a weekly or monthly basis. This amount is in addition to tithes and regular offerings. It focuses on what God will supply for the faith promise. The amount to give is decided on through individual prayer.

Read the article provided "What is a Faith Promise?" Use it to prepare and challenge students regarding a faith promise. Set a goal to have 100 percent participation from the group, no matter how small the pledge. Also, set a realistic goal of how much you feel students can give for the year.

Gather materials and share this concept with your youth workers. Have a calculator or adding machine on hand to count up the pledges that are made during this activity.

## Method

Explain the concept of a faith promise. Distribute the pledge forms and pencils. Lead in prayer, followed by a time of silent, individual prayer during which young people establish the amount of their faith promise.

Collect the pledge forms and have someone add up the yearly totals immediately.

Announce the totals. At that point, depending on the situation, you may want to ask if anyone would like to make additional pledges.

In the following weeks, at the offering, remind students about their faith promises. Have them give it separate from their tithe or designate it for "missions." Keep track of the amount of faith promises that come in during the year. At the end of the year, when you are ready to have students make another faith promise, you can give them the previous year's results.

# What is a Faith Promise?

by

Joyce Wells Booze

In a missions convention a small boy filled out a faith promise card. He printed his name and address and promised to give 25 cents per month for missions. Then across the bottom of the card in uneven block letters, he printed: "My daddy will pay this."

That statement captures the spirit of faith promise giving. A faith promise is based not on your known resources, but on faith in what your Heavenly Father will do. It is promising to give to missions what you believe God is going to supply.

Faith promises are usually received during a missions convention or a missionary service. The pastor gives each person a card and asks him to fill in his name and how much he believes God would have him give to missions each month for the coming year. By totaling up all the promises, the pastor can determine your church's missions goal for the year.

There are several important truths that should be understood about faith promises. First, a faith promise is made according to your faith. You promise to give what God provides. It is not a pledge. Pledges are made on the basis of what you foresee as possible for you to do from your known income.

Second, a faith promise is an agreement between you and God. No one will come to collect it. Your promise represents a personal goal of what you want to attempt for God.

Third, a faith promise is a plan for giving in addition to your regular tithes and offerings. A tithe is the one-tenth of your income that belongs to God. Offerings are your gifts above your tithes for special needs or projects. As Christians are faithful in giving their tithes and offerings, the operational needs of the church are met. Faith promise giving is a step beyond tithes and offerings; it is believing God to supply funds that you as a steward can give toward reaching the world with the gospel.

Fourth, faith promise giving enables every Christian to have a part in fulfilling the Great Commission. The command of Jesus, "Go ye into all the world, and preach the gospel" (Mark 16:15), is not directed just to those whom God calls as ministers. Spreading the gospel is the responsibility of every believer. Most laymen want to be a part of reaching the world for Christ but they don't know what they can do. Faith promise giving allows everyone to participate in the missionary endeavor of the church.

Faith promise giving emphasizes not what you have to give, but what you believe God to supply. If you feel that your faith is weak, you have every right to ask God to increase it. Of course, committing to God what we already have in our possession prepares us to believe Him for additional resources.

One of the exciting things about faith promise giving is that it enriches the life of the giver. His faith stretches past its former boundaries into areas he hasn't claimed before. The excitement of having God supply the funds to pay the faith promise encourages the giver to believe for spiritual and physical needs as well as material.

Faith promise giving can also revitalize churches. Testimonies from congregation after congregation reveal that they have received both financial and spiritual blessings because of the excitement and faith generated in their midst by the church uniting in faith promise giving. This faith has enabled many churches to be of greater service in their own communities than they would have dared to believe possible before they experienced the adventure of faith promise giving.

Dr. Oswald J. Smith, who led the People's Church in Toronto, Canada, to become the greatest missions-giving church in the world, did so by using the faith promise plan. He says, "If I had waited until I had cash, I would not have given at all. But I gave when I didn't have it. I gave when I had to trust God for it."

A faith promise is a means of giving to God when we don't have anything to give. How much can you trust your Heavenly Father to channel through you to reach the multitudes that He loves and yearns over?

Give, and it shall be given unto you; good measure, pressed down, and shaken together, and running over. . . . For with the same measure that ye mete withal it shall be measured to you again. (Luke 6:38)

# My Financial Faith Promise

As God enables me, I will express my faith and help reach my generation with the gospel by giving to the missions program of my local church as I have indicated.

I understand this financial Faith Promise is a covenant between God and me. I will not be asked for payment at any time.

My Faith Promise

☐ $5    ☐ $30

☐ $10   ☐ $50

☐ $15   ☐ $75

☐ $20   ☐ $100

☐ $25   ☐ $____

This is a

☐ Weekly Faith Promise

☐ Monthly Faith Promise

I would like to make a one-time gift of $_____

My total* Faith Promise $_____

*(*To get this total, multiply your Faith Promise by the number of weeks or months and add your one-time gift.)*

Name _____

Address _____

City/State/Zip _____

Signature _____

# TOPICAL INDEX

# Recommended Reading List

Barrett, David B., and Todd M. Johnson. *Our Globe and How to Reach It: Seeing the World Evangelized by A.D. 2000 and Beyond.* Birmingham, Ala.: New Hope, 1990.

Barrett, David B., ed. *World Christian Encyclopedia: A Comparative Survey of Churches and Religions in the Modern World, A.D. 1900–2000.* Nairobi: Oxford University Press, 1982.

Jansen, Frank Kaleb, ed. *Target Earth: The Necessity of Diversity in a Holistic Perspective on World Mission.* Pasadena, California: University of the Nations/Hawaii and Global Mapping International, 1989.

Johnstone, P. J. *Operation World: A Handbook for World Intercession.* Tulsa: STL Books, 1978. Reprint 1983.

# Notes

[1] Sources: See recommended reading list above.

[2] Frank Kaleb Jansen, ed., *Target Earth: The Necessity of Diversity in a Holistic Perspective on World Mission* (Pasadena, California: University of the Nations/Hawaii and Global Mapping International, 1989), 19.

[3] David B. Barrett and Todd M. Johnson, *Our Globe and How to Reach It: Seeing the World Evangelized by A.D. 2000 and Beyond* (Birmingham, Ala.: New Hope,1990), 24, 28.

[4] Ibid., 24, 25, and 36.

[5] See recommended reading list above.

[6] See recommended reading list above.